David, the boy, soothed the king with music and killed the giant with a sling.
David, the towering king, loved God and was wise. But his desire for a beautiful woman—another man's wife—led to the death of his infant son . . . and deep sorrow for his sin. Another son betrayed him.
Yet, when Solomon became king, he too was first wise—then foolish. He permitted idol worship to please his wives . . . and turned Israel into a nation divided against itself. But one of God's prophets—Elijah—worked a miracle when the priests of Baal could not, and brought glory to the one true God where before there had been division, chaos, and murder.

Here is the third in the unique series that brings all of the excitement, drama and color of the Bible in words and pictures from the world's greatest, truest Book!

The Picture Bible for All Ages

VOLUME 3

KINGS AND PROPHETS

1 SAMUEL 16: 23—1 KINGS 21: 8

Script by Iva Hoth

Illustrations by Andre Le Blanc

Bible Editor, C. Elvan Olmstead, Ph.D.

David C. Cook Publishing Co.
850 NORTH GROVE AVENUE • ELGIN, IL 60120
In Canada: David C. Cook Publishing (Canada) Ltd., Weston, Ontario M9L 1T4

KINGS AND PROPHETS
First printing, June 1973
© 1973 David C. Cook Publishing Co., Elgin, IL 60120
All Rights Reserved. This book, or parts thereof,
may not be reproduced in any form without permission
of the publisher, except by a reviewer who wishes
to quote brief passages in connection with a review
in a magazine or newspaper.
Published by David C. Cook Publishing Co.
Printed in United States of America by Offset Paperbacks.
Library of Congress Catalog Card Number: 73-78170
ISBN: 0-912692-15-4

ILLUSTRATED STORIES

KINGS AND PROPHETS

We will have a king . . .
That we also may be
like all the nations.
And the Lord said to Samuel,
Hearken unto their voice,
and make them a king.
. . . and he shall know that
there is a prophet in Israel.

I SAMUEL 8: 19, 20, 22;
II KINGS 5: 8

A Giant's Challenge

FROM I SAMUEL 16: 23—17: 26

TWICE KING SAUL DELIBERATELY DISOBEYS GOD. THE PROPHET, SAMUEL, HAS TOLD HIM THAT HIS KINGDOM WILL BE TAKEN FROM HIM. SAUL IS AFRAID—AND AT TIMES HIS MIND BECOMES UNBALANCED. WHEN HIS ADVISORS TELL HIM ABOUT DAVID, A YOUNG SHEPHERD, WHO SINGS AND PLAYS A HARP, SAUL SENDS FOR HIM. DAVID ARRIVES AT THE PALACE...

THE KING IS VERY ILL TODAY—SO HE MAY BE DANGEROUS. NEVER TAKE YOUR EYES OFF HIM.

QUIETLY DAVID ENTERS THE KING'S ROOM AND BEGINS TO PLAY... SAUL STARES AT HIM WILDLY... BUT DAVID CONTINUES TO PLAY AND SING OF HIS FAITH IN GOD.

AT LAST KING SAUL RELAXES AND FALLS QUIETLY ASLEEP. AFTER THAT DAVID IS OFTEN CALLED TO THE PALACE. HIS MUSIC QUIETS SAUL'S TORTURED MIND—AND IN TIME THE KING SEEMS WELL AGAIN.

AND WHEN WORD COMES THAT THE PHILISTINES ARE PREPARING FOR AN ATTACK, SAUL LEADS HIS ARMY AGAINST THEM. DAVID'S THREE OLDEST BROTHERS JOIN THE KING'S FORCES.

ONE EVENING DAVID COMES IN FROM THE FIELDS TO FIND HIS FATHER BUSY PACKING FOOD.

THIS IS FOR YOUR BROTHERS. I WANT YOU TO TAKE IT TO THEM.

I'LL LEAVE RIGHT AWAY. WHAT'S THE LATEST NEWS FROM THE FRONT?

NOT GOOD, AND I'M WORRIED.

WHEN DAVID REACHES THE ISRAELITE CAMP, HE FINDS THE SOLDIERS STRANGELY QUIET.

WHAT'S THE MATTER?

THE MATTER? LISTEN TO THAT GIANT!

SEND OUT A MAN WHO DARES TO FIGHT ME. IF HE KILLS ME, THE PHILISTINES WILL BE YOUR SERVANTS, BUT IF I KILL HIM, YOU WILL BE OUR SERVANTS.

WHO IS THAT PHILISTINE THAT HE CAN DEFY THE ARMY OF GOD?

THAT'S THE GIANT, GOLIATH— THE BIGGEST, STRONGEST, MOST FEARED OF ALL THE PHILISTINE SOLDIERS. NO MAN DARES TO TAKE UP HIS CHALLENGE.

NO MAN? IS EVERY ISRAELITE SOLDIER A COWARD?

THOSE ARE STRONG WORDS, BOY. BUT—LOOK —HERE COMES YOUR BIG BROTHER. YOU'D BETTER GET OUT OF HERE BEFORE HE HEARS WHAT YOU'VE SAID.

The Challenge Is Met

FROM I SAMUEL 17: 28-48

WHEN DAVID REACHES THE ISRAELITE CAMP, HE FINDS THAT NO ISRAELITE SOLDIER IS BRAVE ENOUGH TO ACCEPT THE PHILISTINE GIANT'S CHALLENGE TO FIGHT. DAVID IS ANGRY—BUT SO IS ELIAB, HIS BIG BROTHER...

WHAT ARE **YOU** DOING HERE? WHY AREN'T YOU HOME WHERE YOU BELONG—TAKING CARE OF THE SHEEP?

FATHER SENT ME HERE WITH FOOD FOR YOU—NOW **YOU** TELL ME WHY NO ONE HAS ACCEPTED GOLIATH'S CHALLENGE TO FIGHT?

EVER SINCE THE PROPHET SAMUEL CHOSE DAVID INSTEAD OF HIM, ELIAB HAS BEEN FILLED WITH JEALOUSY...NOW IT BURSTS INTO THE OPEN.

YOU'RE JUST A SHOW-OFF.

I'M NOT AFRAID. I'LL FIGHT THE GIANT.

MEANWHILE IN KING SAUL'S TENT...

EVERY DAY THAT GIANT DEFIES US. I HAVE OFFERED A HANDSOME REWARD—EVEN MY DAUGHTER IN MARRIAGE—BUT NOT ONE SOLDIER IN MY WHOLE ARMY WILL ACCEPT THE CHALLENGE.

O KING—THERE IS ONE OUTSIDE WHO ACCEPTS, BUT—

BRING HIM HERE AT ONCE!

DAVID ENTERS—BUT SAUL DOES NOT REMEMBER THE SHEPHERD WHO PLAYED FOR HIM.

A SHEPHERD BOY! YOU CAN'T FIGHT A GIANT!

THE LORD WHO HELPED ME KILL A LION AND A BEAR WILL HELP ME NOW.

MAYBE YOU'RE RIGHT—AT LEAST YOU HAVE COURAGE. GO, AND THE LORD BE WITH THEE. YOU CAN WEAR MY OWN ARMOR.

I CAN'T WEAR THIS—I'M NOT USED TO FIGHTING IN ARMOR. BESIDES, MY PLAN IS NOT TO DEFEND MYSELF, BUT TO ATTACK!

14

The Jealous King

FROM I SAMUEL 17: 48—18: 9

FOR FORTY DAYS THE PHILISTINE GIANT, GOLIATH, CHALLENGES THE ISRAELITES TO FIGHT. BUT NOT ONE SOLDIER IN ALL OF KING SAUL'S ARMY IS BRAVE ENOUGH TO ACCEPT THE CHALLENGE, UNTIL DAVID, THE YOUNG SHEPHERD, OFFERS TO MEET THE GIANT WITH ONLY A STAFF, A SLING—AND HIS FAITH IN GOD! EVEN WHILE DAVID WHIRLS HIS SLING, THE GIANT LAUGHS, BUT THE STONE HITS ITS MARK...AND THE GIANT FALLS!

GOLIATH'S DEAD!

IN TERROR, THE PHILISTINES FLEE FOR THEIR LIVES. SPURRED ON BY THIS SUDDEN TURN OF EVENTS, THE EXCITED ISRAELITES CHASE THE PHILISTINES BACK TO THEIR OWN LAND.

WHEN THE ARMY RETURNS, SAUL'S GENERAL, ABNER, TAKES DAVID TO SEE THE KING.

YOU SAVED ISRAEL, DAVID. FROM NOW ON YOU WILL LIVE IN THE PALACE. PRINCE JONATHAN WILL TAKE YOU BACK WITH HIM.

DAVID AND JONATHAN BECOME TRUE FRIENDS— AND MAKE A PACT OF FRIENDSHIP.

DAVID, I'M PROUD TO BE THE FRIEND OF THE BRAVEST MAN IN ISRAEL. I WANT TO GIVE YOU MY ROBE AND ARMOR AS A SIGN THAT I WILL BE LOYAL TO YOU—FOREVER!

THANK YOU, JONATHAN. GOD IS MY WITNESS THAT I WILL BE YOUR FRIEND UNTIL DEATH.

TRIUMPHANTLY, KING SAUL AND HIS VICTORIOUS SOLDIERS RETURN HOME...THE WOMEN RUSH OUT OF THE CITIES TO GREET THEM AND SING THEIR PRAISES.

SAUL HAS SLAIN HIS THOUSANDS—AND DAVID HIS TEN THOUSANDS!

WHEN SAUL HEARS THESE WORDS, HE THINKS OF WHAT THE PROPHET SAMUEL TOLD HIM: "BECAUSE YOU HAVE DISOBEYED GOD, YOUR KINGDOM WILL BE GIVEN TO ANOTHER."

THE PEOPLE KNOW DAVID IS A GREATER WARRIOR THAN I. MAYBE *HE'S* THE ONE WHO WILL TAKE MY KINGDOM FROM ME!

THAT NIGHT SAUL CANNOT SLEEP.

DAVID! HE'S THE HERO NOW! BUT HE CAN'T TAKE MY KINGDOM FROM ME—IF HE'S DEAD!

Plot to Kill

FROM I SAMUEL 18: 10—19: 11

WHEN THE PEOPLE SING THEIR PRAISES TO DAVID, SAUL BECOMES JEALOUS. HIS JEALOUSY DRIVES HIM ALMOST MAD AS HE THINKS THAT DAVID MIGHT BE THE ONE WHO WILL TAKE HIS KINGDOM FROM HIM. TO SAUL THERE IS ONLY ONE ANSWER—GET RID OF DAVID!

NO MAN CAN TAKE MY KINGDOM FROM ME!

THE KING'S INSANE!

LET'S CALL DAVID—HIS MUSIC HELPED THE KING BEFORE!

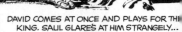

DAVID COMES AT ONCE AND PLAYS FOR THE KING. SAUL GLARES AT HIM STRANGELY... TOYS WITH HIS SPEAR...

...THEN HURLS IT STRAIGHT AT DAVID. BUT DAVID IS TOO QUICK... HE DODGES THE SPEAR AND ESCAPES.

A FEW DAYS LATER SAUL MAKES ANOTHER ATTEMPT TO KILL DAVID. BUT AGAIN HE MISSES. FINALLY HE HAS A NEW IDEA...

MAYBE IT'S BEST THAT I DON'T KILL DAVID. THE PEOPLE MIGHT TURN AGAINST ME. I MUST MAKE HIS DEATH LOOK ACCIDENTAL— OR IN BATTLE. THAT'S IT— IN BATTLE!

SAUL'S CHANCE COMES SOONER THAN HE EXPECTS...

PRINCESS MICHAL IS IN LOVE WITH DAVID, BUT DAVID SAYS HE IS TOO POOR TO MARRY THE DAUGHTER OF A KING.

TELL DAVID THAT THE ONLY GIFT I WANT FROM HIM IS ONE HUNDRED DEAD PHILISTINES.

THIS IS BETTER THAN I HAD HOPED.

DAVID LOVES MICHAL, SO TO FULFILL THE KING'S DEMAND, HE MAKES A SURPRISE RAID AGAINST A PHILISTINE CAMP AND KILLS 200 PHILISTINES... LATER AT THE WEDDING OF PRINCESS MICHAL AND DAVID EVERYONE REJOICES— EXCEPT SAUL.

HE IS MORE POPULAR THAN EVER. I CAN'T WAIT FOR AN ACCIDENT TO HAPPEN. I'LL **ORDER** HIM KILLED.

SAUL CALLS HIS OFFICERS AND JONATHAN TO HIM AND ORDERS THEM TO PUT DAVID TO DEATH.

BUT, FATHER, HE RISKED HIS LIFE TO SAVE US. WHY DO YOU WANT TO KILL AN INNOCENT MAN?

YOU ARE RIGHT. AS THE LORD LIVES, DAVID SHALL NOT BE KILLED.

DAVID LEADS THE ARMY IN ANOTHER SUCCESSFUL BATTLE AGAINST THE PHILISTINES. SAUL'S JEALOUSY INCREASES... AND IN ANGER HE BREAKS HIS PROMISE.

WATCH DAVID'S HOUSE...IN THE MORNING, WHEN HE LEAVES, **KILL** HIM.

Escape in the Night

FROM I SAMUEL 19: 11-22

KING SAUL IS AFRAID THAT DAVID MIGHT SOME DAY TAKE HIS KINGDOM FROM HIM. SEVERAL TIMES SAUL ATTEMPTS TO KILL DAVID, BUT EACH TIME HE FAILS. NOW HE ORDERS TWO OF HIS MEN TO GO TO DAVID'S HOUSE, AND KILL HIM.

THE JOB MUST BE DONE QUICKLY AND QUIETLY... IF THE PEOPLE FIND OUT WHAT IS GOING ON, THERE WILL BE TROUBLE.

YOU'RE RIGHT— DAVID GETS MORE POPULAR EVERY DAY.

BUT EVEN AS SAUL'S MEN PLAN THEIR EVIL WORK, MICHAL WARNS HER HUSBAND...

I HAVE LEARNED THAT MY FATHER PLANS TO KILL YOU. YOU MUST ESCAPE BEFORE DAYLIGHT.

BUT HE PROMISED JONATHAN HE WOULDN'T HARM ME.

THEN HE HAS CHANGED HIS MIND AGAIN—HIS MEN ARE ON THEIR WAY HERE RIGHT NOW. YOU MUST LEAVE BY THE BACK WINDOW. PLEASE—DAVID— BEFORE IT IS TOO LATE.

21

HURRY—I HAVE A PLAN THAT WILL DELAY THE MEN AND GIVE YOU TIME.

GOD BLESS YOU, MICHAL. I'LL SEND WORD TO YOU WHEN I CAN.

QUICKLY MICHAL PLACES A DUMMY IN THE BED AND COVERS IT. IN THE MORNING...

WE HAVE A MESSAGE FROM THE KING FOR DAVID.

HE'S SICK— SEE, HE'S IN BED.

MICHAL'S SCHEME WORKS—THE MEN LEAVE. AT THE PALACE THEY REPORT TO KING SAUL.

WE COULDN'T GET TO DAVID—YOUR DAUGHTER SAID HE WAS SICK IN BED.

THEN BRING HIM TO ME IN HIS BED—I'LL KILL HIM MYSELF!

SAUL'S MEN RETURN TO DAVID'S HOUSE. THEY COME IN AND PREPARE TO TAKE DAVID BY FORCE...

A DUMMY!

WHERE IS DAVID?

HE'S GONE— I DON'T KNOW WHERE.

SAUL IS FURIOUS! BUT HE CAN DO NOTHING...UNTIL ONE DAY HE LEARNS THAT DAVID IS STAYING WITH THE PROPHET, SAMUEL, IN THE CITY OF RAMAH. SAUL SENDS MEN TO CAPTURE DAVID, BUT WHEN THEY DO NOT RETURN, SAUL SENDS A MESSENGER TO FIND OUT WHY.

WHAT HAPPENED? QUICK, MAN, SPEAK UP!

WHEN YOUR MEN REACHED THE TOWN WHERE DAVID IS THEY FOUND SAMUEL LEADING THE PROPHETS IN PRAISING GOD. YOUR MEN JOINED THEM—MAYBE GOD WARNED THEM NOT TO HARM DAVID...

EXCUSES! THAT'S ALL I HEAR. IF THERE'S NO ONE BRAVE ENOUGH TO CARRY OUT MY COMMAND, I'LL DO IT MYSELF!

The Angry King
FROM I SAMUEL 19: 22—20: 33

I'LL KILL HIM MYSELF! DAVID MAY BE A HERO TO THE PEOPLE, BUT HE WON'T LIVE TO TAKE _MY_ KINGDOM FROM ME!

THREE TIMES SAUL SENDS MEN TO RAMAH TO CAPTURE DAVID. BUT EACH TIME THE MEN FAIL. IN A FIT OF RAGE, SAUL SETS OUT...

—BUT ON THE WAY A STRANGE THING HAPPENS...

GOD TAKES CONTROL OF SAUL. AND WHEN SAUL REACHES RAMAH HE FALLS TO THE GROUND AND LIES THERE FOR A DAY AND A NIGHT.

WHILE SAUL IS IN RAMAH, DAVID HURRIES BACK TO THE PALACE TO SEE HIS FRIEND, PRINCE JONATHAN

INSIDE THE PALACE DAVID SEEKS OUT HIS FRIEND.

DAVID! WHAT BRINGS YOU BACK HERE?

I MUST KNOW WHY YOUR FATHER WANTS TO KILL ME. COME—LET'S GO WHERE WE CAN TALK WITHOUT BEING HEARD.

MY FATHER MEANS YOU NO HARM, DAVID. HE WOULD TELL ME IF HE DID.

NO, JONATHAN. HE WOULD NOT TELL YOU BECAUSE YOU ARE MY FRIEND.

TOMORROW STARTS THE KING'S FEAST OF THE NEW MOON—BUT I WON'T ATTEND. IF YOUR FATHER ASKS ABOUT ME, TELL HIM I HAVE GONE TO BETHLEHEM TO SEE MY FAMILY. IF HE IS NOT ANGRY, THEN ALL IS WELL. BUT IF HE IS—REMEMBER THE AGREEMENT WE MADE BEFORE GOD TO BE FRIENDS, ALWAYS.

I'LL FIND OUT THE TRUTH. NOW, LET'S GO OUT IN THE FIELD WHERE WE CAN SET UP A SECRET PLAN FOR ME TO LET YOU KNOW HOW MY FATHER FEELS.

JONATHAN AND DAVID MAKE THEIR PLANS, THEN—

WHATEVER HAPPENS, DAVID, THE LORD IS A WITNESS TO OUR AGREEMENT THAT WE WILL BE LOYAL TO EACH OTHER—AND TO EACH OTHER'S CHILDREN.

YES, NOTHING WILL EVER BREAK UP OUR FRIENDSHIP. GOOD-BY.

ON THE SECOND DAY OF THE KING'S FEAST—

WHERE'S DAVID?

HE ASKED TO VISIT HIS FAMILY IN BETHLEHEM —I LET HIM GO.

DON'T YOU KNOW THAT AS LONG AS DAVID LIVES YOU WILL NEVER BE KING? BRING HIM HERE, FOR HE MUST DIE!

WHY SHOULD HE BE KILLED? WHAT HAS HE DONE BUT SERVE YOU WELL IN BATTLE?

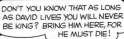

EVEN MY OWN SON IS FOR DAVID.

WHEN PRINCE JONATHAN DEFENDS DAVID, KING SAUL GOES MAD WITH RAGE. IN FRONT OF ALL HIS GUESTS HE HURLS A SPEAR AT HIS OWN SON. JONATHAN DODGES—AND THE SPEAR STRIKES THE WALL.

TRAITOR!

HE'S INSANE! AND HE WILL NEVER REST UNTIL HE HAS KILLED DAVID.

EARLY THE NEXT MORNING JONATHAN CARRIES OUT HIS SECRET AGREEMENT WITH DAVID. HE HURRIES TO THE FIELD WHERE DAVID IS HIDING.

LOOK, BOY, THAT ARROW IS **BEYOND** YOU.

BEYOND! THAT'S THE SIGNAL. IT MEANS DEATH FOR ME IF I GO BACK TO THE PALACE!

GOD HELPED ME WHEN I KILLED GOLIATH. HE WILL HELP ME NOW IF I TRUST AND OBEY HIM.

AFRAID THAT HE HAS BEEN SEEN AT THE TABERNACLE, DAVID KEEPS ON THE MOVE. HE CROSSES THE BORDER INTO THE LAND OF THE PHILISTINES.

I SHOULD BE SAFE HERE FOR A WHILE—SAUL WOULD NOT DARE TO LOOK FOR ME IN ENEMY COUNTRY.

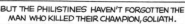

BUT THE PHILISTINES HAVEN'T FORGOTTEN THE MAN WHO KILLED THEIR CHAMPION, GOLIATH.

THAT'S DAVID—

WHAT'S HE DOING IN OUR COUNTRY? A SPY, MAYBE...

LET'S WARN THE KING!

29

OUR BIBLE IN PICTURES

Trapped in a Cave

FROM I SAMUEL 21: 13—24: 5

FORCED TO FLEE FOR HIS LIFE FROM KING SAUL, DAVID TRIES TO FIND SAFETY IN ENEMY COUNTRY. BUT SOME OF THE PHILISTINES REMEMBER DAVID AND WARN THEIR KING AGAINST HIM. TO FOOL THEM, DAVID PRETENDS HE IS CRAZY.

THIS IS DAVID, THE ISRAELITE WHO KILLED GOLIATH.

HE'S MAD! TAKE THAT CRAZY MAN OUT OF MY SIGHT!

DAVID RETURNS TO ISRAEL....AND THE NEWS OF HIS WHEREABOUTS SPREADS QUICKLY AMONG HIS FRIENDS.

KING SAUL HAS ORDERED US TO FIGHT **AGAINST** YOU— BUT WE WANT TO FIGHT **FOR** YOU.

GOOD. THAT MAKES FOUR HUNDRED MEN ON OUR SIDE.

BUT NEWS ABOUT DAVID ALSO REACHES SAUL.

THE PRIESTS AT NOB. ARE HELPING DAVID. ONE OF THEM GAVE HIM GOLIATH'S SWORD. I SAW THE WHOLE THING WITH MY OWN EYES.

BRING THE PRIESTS TO ME—I'LL MAKE AN EXAMPLE OF TRAITORS WHO HELP DAVID.

THE PRIESTS OF NOB PLEAD INNOCENT TO THE CHARGE OF PLOTTING AGAINST SAUL—BUT HE WILL NOT LISTEN!

YOU HELPED MY ENEMY—AND FOR THIS YOU WILL DIE!

IN HIS INSANE DESIRE FOR REVENGE, SAUL ORDERS THE DEATH OF NOT ONLY THE PRIESTS OF NOB, BUT OF EVERY MAN, WOMAN AND CHILD IN THEIR CITY. ONLY ONE MAN ESCAPES, ABIATHAR...

...WHO CARRIES THE TRAGIC NEWS TO DAVID.

GOD FORGIVE ME. I AM PARTLY TO BLAME. I ASKED FOR HELP, AND YOUR FATHER GAVE IT. STAY WITH ME—FOR NOW SAUL SEEKS YOUR LIFE AS WELL AS MINE.

REPORTS OF DAVID'S MOVEMENTS ARE AGAIN BROUGHT TO SAUL—AND THIS TIME THE JEALOUS KING SETS OUT WITH THREE THOUSAND MEN.

BUT DAVID'S SCOUTS ARE ON THE ALERT...

SAUL AND HIS SOLDIERS ARE HEADED THIS WAY—THEY OUTNUMBER US MORE THAN SEVEN TO ONE.

WE CAN'T RISK A FIGHT! QUICK—HIDE IN HERE.

A FEW MINUTES LATER, SAUL, TIRED FROM HIS HARD RIDE, STOPS TO REST—IN THE VERY CAVE WHERE DAVID AND HIS MEN ARE HIDING!

INSIDE, EAGER EYES WATCH THE KING'S EVERY MOVEMENT.

GOD HAS PLACED THE KING IN YOUR POWER.

LET ME KILL HIM.

STAY BACK— I'LL TAKE CARE OF THIS.

Revenge

FROM I SAMUEL 24: 5—25: 13

WHY DOESN'T DAVID KILL HIM?

HE JUST STANDS THERE!

AFRAID THAT DAVID WILL TAKE HIS KINGDOM FROM HIM, KING SAUL SETS OUT WITH HIS ARMY TO CAPTURE DAVID. ON THE WAY HE STOPS TO REST IN A CAVE—UNAWARE THAT DAVID AND HIS MEN ARE HIDING IN THE BACK OF IT.

DAVID LOOKS DOWN AT THE KING—AND THINKS OF ALL THE TIMES SAUL HAS TRIED TO KILL HIM. NOW THE JEALOUS KING IS AT HIS MERCY—BUT DAVID ONLY BENDS DOWN AND CAREFULLY CUTS OFF A PIECE OF THE ROYAL ROBE.

HE'S YOUR WIFE'S FATHER—SO IF YOU DON'T WANT TO KILL HIM, I'LL DO IT FOR YOU.

NO—HE WAS CHOSEN BY GOD TO BE OUR KING. IT IS NOT FOR US TO DECIDE WHEN HE WILL DIE.

AFTER A TIME SAUL LEAVES THE CAVE—AND DAVID CALLS AFTER HIM.

MY LORD THE KING.

DAVID!

WHY DO YOU KEEP HUNTING ME? I MEAN YOU NO HARM. SEE THIS PIECE OF CLOTH? I CUT IT FROM YOUR ROBE. I COULD HAVE KILLED YOU, BUT I DIDN'T.

I AM ASHAMED. YOU ARE A BETTER MAN THAN I AM, DAVID. I WILL GO NOW AND LEAVE YOU ALONE.

SAUL LEADS HIS ARMY AWAY ...BUT A SHORT TIME LATER DAVID LEARNS THAT SAUL HAS FORCED MICHAL, DAVID'S WIFE, TO MARRY ANOTHER MAN. DAVID KNOWS NOW THAT SAUL IS STILL ANGRY AND THAT HE WILL NEVER BE SAFE AS LONG AS SAUL LIVES. WORD COMES, TOO, THAT HIS OLD FRIEND, SAMUEL, THE PROPHET, IS DEAD.

34

SAD AND WEARY, DAVID LEADS HIS MEN OUT INTO THE WILDERNESS. BUT AFTER A TIME...

WE'RE RUNNING OUT OF FOOD. DO YOU KNOW WHERE WE CAN GET SOME?

A MAN NAMED NABAL LIVES NEAR HERE. HE'S RICH— MAYBE HE WILL HELP US.

AT NABAL'S SHEEPFOLD...

DAVID HAS BEEN PROTECTING THE FLOCKS OF THIS AREA FROM BANDITS. NOW HE NEEDS YOUR HELP— WE HAVE COME TO ASK FOR FOOD.

FOOD? WHY SHOULD I FEED DAVID OR HIS MEN? GO AWAY.

THE MESSENGERS' REPORT ANGERS DAVID.

CALL UP FOUR HUNDRED OF OUR MEN—TELL THEM TO ARM THEMSELVES FOR A RAID.

Spies in the Night

FROM I SAMUEL 25: 13—26: 6

IN A BURST OF ANGER DAVID SETS OUT TO PUNISH NABAL, THE MAN WHO REFUSED TO SEND HIM FOOD. BUT ON THE WAY HE MEETS A WOMAN WITH A CARAVAN OF FOOD. AT THE SIGHT OF DAVID SHE DISMOUNTS AND BOWS BEFORE HIM...

I AM ABIGAIL, THE WIFE OF NABAL.

I HAVE BROUGHT FOOD FOR YOU AND YOUR MEN. I PRAY DO NOT TAKE REVENGE ON NABAL AND HAVE HIS BLOOD ON YOUR HANDS. YOU ARE FIGHTING THE BATTLES OF THE LORD—LET NO EVIL BE FOUND IN YOU.

GOD BLESS YOU, ABIGAIL. THE LORD MUST HAVE SENT YOU TO STOP ME FROM WHAT I MEANT TO DO TO NABAL. GO IN PEACE.

36

ABIGAIL RETURNS HOME TO FIND NABAL CELEBRATING THE END OF THE SHEARING OF THE SHEEP. HE IS SO DRUNK THAT ABIGAIL DOES NOT TELL HIM WHAT SHE HAS DONE...

UNTIL THE NEXT MORNING.

WHAT? YOU TOOK **MY** FOOD TO THAT REBEL? HOW DARE YOU—

BUT NABAL'S BURST OF ANGER IS CUT SHORT. HE HAS A STROKE— AND TEN DAYS LATER HE DIES.

TIME THE NEWS OF NABAL'S DEATH REACHES DAVID...

THANK GOD OR KEEPING ME FROM DOING EVIL.

WONDER HAT WILL COME OF ABIGAIL?

DAVID CONTINUES TO THINK OF ABIGAIL— OF HER BEAUTY AND HER KINDNESS TO HIM. HE SENDS MESSENGERS TO HER...

DAVID HAS SENT US TO ASK YOU TO BECOME HIS WIFE.

I AM HONORED TO BE CHOSEN BY DAVID.

AT HIS CAMP IN THE WILDERNESS OF ZIPH, DAVID WAITS ANXIOUSLY FOR ABIGAIL'S ARRIVAL.

ABIGAIL AND DAVID ARE MARRIED, BUT THE FEASTING IS SCARCELY OVER WHEN ONE OF DAVID'S SCOUTS BRINGS A WARNING...

KING SAUL AND THREE THOUSAND SOLDIERS ARE PITCHING CAMP IN THE VALLEY— THEY PLAN TO ATTACK US!

SHOW WHE THE AR

WHERE IS KING SAUL?

SAFE IN THE CENTER— SURROUNDED BY ALL OF HIS SOLDIERS. NO MAN COULD BREAK INTO THAT CAMP —AND COME OUT ALIVE!

David's Dilemma

FROM I SAMUEL 26: 6—28: 2

KING SAUL AND HIS ARMY ARE CAMPED IN THE VALLEY—PREPARING TO ATTACK DAVID. BUT DAVID IS WARNED, AND IN THE DARK OF NIGHT HE AND HIS YOUNG NEPHEW, ABISHAI, STEAL PAST THE SLEEPING GUARDS IN SEARCH OF THE KING. ONE FALSE MOVE AND THE WHOLE CAMP WILL BE AROUSED...

STEALTHILY THEY CREEP UP BESIDE THE SLEEPING KING.

GOD HAS PUT YOUR ENEMY IN OUR HANDS. I'LL PIN HIM TO THE GROUND WITH ONE BLOW.

NO! THE LORD ANOINTED SAUL KING OF ISRAEL, AND THE LORD WILL DECIDE WHEN AND HOW SAUL IS TO DIE.

HAND ME HIS SPEAR AND WATER JUG. THEN WE'LL LEAVE THE SAME WAY WE CAME INTO CAMP.

THE NEXT MORNING DAVID CALLS DOWN TO SAUL'S CAMP.

KING SAUL! LOOK! I HAVE YOUR SPEAR AND WATER JUG!

YOU TOOK THEM WHILE I SLEPT! AGAIN YOU COULD HAVE KILLED ME— AND YOU DIDN'T. I HAVE BEEN A FOOL! I'LL NEVER TRY TO HARM YOU AGAIN.

ASHAMED, KING SAUL ORDERS HIS MEN TO BREAK CAMP AND RETURN HOME.

LOOK! THEY'RE LEAVING—YOU'RE SAFE!

NO—SAUL PROMISED THAT BEFORE. I'LL NEVER BE SAFE AS LONG AS THE KING LIVES.

AND I'M TIRED OF BEING HUNTED LIKE AN OUTLAW. I'M GOING BACK TO THE LAND OF THE PHILISTINES.

PHILISTINES! BUT, UNCLE DAVID, THEY'RE ENEMIES OF ISRAEL. THEY'LL KILL YOU ON SIGHT.

40

41

DAVID IS ON THE SPOT! KING ACHISH HAS ORDERED HIM TO JOIN THE ATTACK ON KING SAUL AND HIS OWN PEOPLE. IF HE REFUSES, THE PHILISTINES WILL TURN ON HIM. SO—AGAINST HIS WILL—HE JOINS THE MARCH AGAINST ISRAEL.

O GOD—HELP ME SO THAT I WILL NOT HAVE TO FIGHT SAUL AND JONATHAN.

UNKNOWN TO DAVID, SOME OF THE PHILISTINE LEADERS ARE HOPING TO KEEP HIM OUT OF THE FIGHT—FOR ANOTHER REASON. THAT NIGHT THEY GO TO KING ACHISH'S TENT.

I DON'T LIKE HAVING DAVID AND HIS MEN BRINGING UP THE REAR. REMEMBER, DAVID IS AN ISRAELITE.

43

44

Voice from the Dead

M I SAMUEL 28: 11-25; 30: 1-3; 31: 1-6

SAUL IS TERRIFIED BY THE SIGHT OF THE APPROACHING PHILISTINE ARMY. IN DESPERATION, HE DISGUISES HIMSELF AND STEALS THROUGH THE NIGHT TO SEEK THE ADVICE OF A WITCH.

CALL UP THE SPIRIT OF THE PROPHET SAMUEL.

FOR A MOMENT ALL IS STILL...THE WOMAN CALLS FOR THE SPIRIT OF SAMUEL. SUDDENLY SHE CRIES OUT IN TERROR...

THEN SAUL HEARS THE VOICE OF SAMUEL: BECAUSE YOU
DISOBEYED GOD, THE LORD WILL DELIVER ISRAEL INTO THE HANDS
OF THE PHILISTINES. TOMORROW YOU AND YOUR SONS WILL BE DEAD.

THE NEXT MORNING THE PHILISTINES ATTACK. ISRAEL, UNDER A WEAK AND FRIGHTENED KING, RETREATS IN PANIC.

THE ENEMY IS EVERYWHERE! WE CAN'T STOP THEM!

MY SONS— WHERE ARE THEY?

DRAW YOUR SWORD AND KILL ME. I WOULD RATHER DIE BY YOUR HAND THAN BE CAPTURED BY THE PHILISTINES.

KILL MY KING? I CAN'T— I CAN'T!

DEAD, SIR.

DEAD! AND I AM BADLY WOUNDED.

SO SAUL DRAWS HIS OWN SWORD— AND FALLS UPON IT.

WHEN THE PEOPLE OF ISRAEL LEARN THAT THEIR KING IS DEAD AND THE ARMY HAS FLED, THEY DESERT THEIR CITIES, LEAVING THEM TO THE CONQUERING PHILISTINES. SO— SAMUEL'S PROPHECY COMES TRUE!

MEANTIME, DAVID AND HIS MEN RIDE TOWARD ZIKLAG...

LOOK! WHAT'S THAT RED GLOW AGAINST THE SKY?

On the Robbers' Trail

FROM I SAMUEL 30: 1-11

DAVID AND HIS MEN RETURN TO FIND THEIR CITY OF ZIKLAG IN SMOLDERING RUINS.

IN VAIN THEY SEARCH THROUGH THE RUBBLE AND ASHES FOR THEIR FAMILIES

49

Front-line News

SO IT WAS THE AMALEKITES WHO RAIDED ZIKLAG? DO YOU KNOW WHERE THEY ARE NOW?

I'LL TAKE YOU TO THEIR CAMP— IF YOU PROMISE NOT TO TURN ME OVER TO MY MASTER. HE'D KILL ME.

DAVID PROMISES. AND, TRUE TO HIS WORD, THE SLAVE GUIDES DAVID TO THE AMALEKITE CAMP— WHERE THE SOLDIERS ARE CELEBRATING THEIR VICTORY.

WE'LL SOON END **THAT** PARTY!

DAVID MAKES A LIGHTNING ATTACK—THE AMALEKITES RALLY THEIR FORCES, BUT THEY ARE NO MATCH FOR COURAGEOUS MEN FIGHTING FOR THEIR WIVES AND CHILDREN.

THE BOOKS OF II SAMUEL AND I CHRONICLES RECORD THE SAME PERIOD OF HISTORY—THE REIGN OF DAVID, ISRAEL'S GREATEST KING. II SAMUEL PRESENTS IT THROUGH THE EYES OF THE PROPHETS, WHILE I CHRONICLES RELATES IT FROM THE VIEWPOINT OF THE PRIESTS.

SOON AFTER DAVID AND HIS MEN RETURN TO ZIKLAG, A MESSENGER COMES WITH NEWS FOR DAVID.

WHO ARE YOU—AND WHAT BRINGS YOU HERE?

I COME FROM THE BATTLE BETWEEN THE PHILISTINES AND ISRAEL. YOUR OLD ENEMY, KING SAUL, IS DEAD—SO IS CROWN PRINCE JONATHAN!

HOW DO YOU KNOW THIS?

I DO NOT KNOW HOW JONATHAN DIED, BUT I FOUND THE KING ON THE BATTLEFIELD. HE WAS INJURED, AND HE ASKED ME TO KILL HIM. I DID— AND HERE ARE HIS CROWN AND BRACELETS TO PROVE IT!

DAVID DOES NOT KNOW THAT THE MAN IS TELLING A LIE, WITH THE HOPE OF RECEIVING A REWARD. FOR A MOMENT HE IS LOST IN GRIEF—THEN HE TURNS IN ANGER UPON THE MAN WHO BROUGHT THE NEWS.

EVEN IF THE KING ASKED YOU TO KILL HIM, YOU HAD NO RIGHT TO TAKE THE LIFE OF THE MAN CHOSEN BY GOD TO BE KING OF ISRAEL. FOR THIS CRIME YOU WILL PAY—WITH YOUR LIFE!

SO THE MAN WHO LIED TO WIN FAVOR WITH DAVID LOSES NOT ONLY THE FAVOR—BUT HIS LIFE!

THEN, BEFORE ALL OF HIS FAITHFUL FOLLOWERS, DAVID SINGS A MEMORIAL SONG FOR JONATHAN AND THE KING.

Song of the Bow

...How are the mighty fallen!...
The bow of Jonathan turned
    not back,
And the sword of Saul
    returned not empty....
In their death they were not
    divided:
They were swifter than eagles,
They were stronger than lions....
I am distressed for thee, my
    brother Jonathan:
Very pleasant hast thou been
    unto me:
Thy love to me was wonderful,
Passing the love of women.
How are the mighty fallen,
And the weapons of war
    perished!

NOW THAT SAUL IS DEAD, DAVID KNOWS THAT HE CAN RETURN TO HIS HOMELAND. BUT BEFORE HE MAKES ANY PLANS, HE PRAYS TO GOD.

LORD, SHALL I RETURN NOW TO MY OWN PEOPLE IN JUDAH?

GOD TELLS DAVID TO RETURN—AND WHEN HE DOES, THE PEOPLE OF JUDAH WELCOME THEIR HERO, AND MAKE HIM KING OF THEIR TRIBE.

GOD BLESS KING DAVID!

LONG LIVE THE KING!

BUT DAVID'S TROUBLES ARE NOT OVER... FOR ACROSS THE JORDAN RIVER SAUL'S YOUNGEST SON, ISHBOSHETH, HAS BEEN CROWNED KING OF THE OTHER TRIBES OF ISRAEL...

WHEN JOAB LEARNS OF ASAHEL'S DEATH, HE IS TORN WITH GRIEF—AND ANGER.

I'LL GET REVENGE!

THE WAR CONTINUES BETWEEN THE TWO KINGDOMS. BUT WITH EACH BATTLE DAVID GROWS STRONGER, AND IN ISH-BOSHETH'S PALACE FEAR AND TENSION MOUNT UNTIL ONE DAY ABNER TURNS ON THE KING...

HOW DARE YOU QUESTION ME? FOR THAT, I WILL TRANSFER MY ALLEGIANCE TO DAVID—AND YOUR KINGDOM WITH IT.

ABNER CARRIES OUT HIS THREAT AND OFFERS TO HELP DAVID ADD THE REST OF ISRAEL TO HIS KINGDOM. DAVID REPLIES WITH AN INVITATION TO A FEAST.

THANK YOU FOR YOUR KINDNESS. I'LL JOIN FORCES WITH YOU... YOU, MY LORD, WILL SOON REIGN OVER ALL ISRAEL!

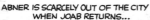

ABNER IS SCARCELY OUT OF THE CITY WHEN JOAB RETURNS...

ABNER JUST LEFT—DAVID HAD A BIG FEAST FOR HIM.

ABNER _HERE_? AND DAVID LET HIM GO?

ANGRILY JOAB RUSHES IN TO SEE DAVID...

DON'T YOU KNOW THAT ABNER CAME HERE AS A SPY—TO FIND OUT YOUR STRENGTH?

DAVID REFUSES TO LISTEN—AND IN A RAGE JOAB STORMS OUT.

I'LL HANDLE THIS _MY_ WAY!

JOAB IS FURIOUS! THIS COULD MEAN TROUBLE!

HE WOULDN'T DARE DEFY THE KING!

Plot Against the King

FROM II SAMUEL 3: 26—4: 5

JOAB IS ANGRY BECAUSE KING DAVID HAS HONORED ABNER, THE GENERAL OF AN ENEMY KING. SECRETLY, JOAB INVITES ABNER TO SEE HIM...

HERE COMES ABNER—THE MAN WHO KILLED MY BROTHER! HE MUST BE WILLING TO BETRAY HIS OWN KING TO WIN FAVOR AND POWER WITH DAVID—MORE POWER THAN I WOULD HAVE!

WHEN ABNER ENTERS THE CITY...

WELCOME, ABNER. I HAVE AN IMPORTANT MATTER TO TAKE UP WITH YOU—WILL YOU STEP OVER HERE WHERE WE CAN TAKE IT UP QUIETLY?

GREETINGS, JOAB. OF COURSE.

JOAB LEADS ABNER TO A QUIET CORNER OF THE BUSY GATE. AND THERE, BEFORE ABNER CAN SUSPECT WHAT IS GOING ON— JOAB STABS HIM. '

DAVID IS ANGRY WHEN HE LEARNS OF ABNER'S MURDER. HE CALLS THE PEOPLE TOGETHER AND ACCUSES JOAB.

THE PUNISHMENT OF JOAB IS IN THE HANDS OF GOD!

TO FURTHER SHOW HIS DISAPPROVAL FOR WHAT JOAB HAS DONE, DAVID LEADS THE MOURNERS IN ABNER'S FUNERAL PROCESSION. BUT EVEN AS KING, DAVID IS NOT SECURE ENOUGH IN HIS NEW KINGDOM TO PUNISH JOAB, FOR JOAB IS THE LEADER OF DAVID'S ARMY.

DAVID MOURNS THE DEATH OF ABNER, BUT ABNER'S MASTER, KING ISH-BOSHETH, IS SHAKEN WITH FRIGHT.

WHAT BAD NEWS! WITHOUT ABNER, I'M LOST.

KING ISH-BOSHETH'S FEARS ARE WELL GROUNDED. FOR EVEN AS HE RECEIVES THE NEWS OF ABNER'S DEATH, TWO OF HIS OWN ARMY OFFICERS ARE PLOTTING...

WITHOUT ABNER, KING ISH-BOSHETH IS A WEAKLING. IF DAVID ATTACKS US, WE'LL BE WIPED OUT.

I HAVE AN IDEA THAT COULD GIVE US POWER —AND A REWARD! LISTEN—JUST THE TWO OF US...

WONDERFUL! LET'S DO IT NOW WHILE IT'S DARK.

NO—IT WILL BE EASIER IF WE JUST WALK INTO THE PALACE IN BROAD DAYLIGHT— AS IF WE WERE GETTING GRAIN. THEN NO ONE WOULD SUSPECT.

AT NOON THE NEXT DAY, WHILE THE KING IS TAKING HIS NAP...

THE REWARD WILL SOON BE OURS!

Hail to the King!

FROM II SAMUEL 4: 6—5: 4

THE KING'S ROOM IS DOWN THIS HALL.

THE WAR AGAINST KING DAVID LEAVES KING ISH-BOSHETH WITH FEW LOYAL FOLLOWERS. IN BROAD DAYLIGHT TWO OF HIS OWN OFFICERS ENTER THE KING'S PALACE...

HE IS ASLEEP.

GOOD—BUT WE MUST ACT SWIFTLY!

BOLDLY THE MEN ENTER THE KING'S BEDROOM AND—WHILE THE PALACE IS RESTING DURING THE HEAT OF THE DAY—THEY KILL HIM. THEN...

63

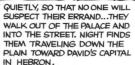

QUIETLY, SO THAT NO ONE WILL SUSPECT THEIR ERRAND...THEY WALK OUT OF THE PALACE AND INTO THE STREET. NIGHT FINDS THEM TRAVELING DOWN THE PLAIN TOWARD DAVID'S CAPITAL IN HEBRON.

BEFORE DAVID THEY PROUDLY TELL THEIR STORY.

WE BRING GOOD NEWS, O KING. **WE** HAVE KILLED YOUR ENEMY, KING ISH-BOSHETH!

WE THOUGHT SOME REWARD...

REWARD! DO YOU THINK I WILL REWARD YOU FOR KILLING AN INNOCENT MAN? THERE'S NO ROOM IN MY KINGDOM FOR TRAITORS WHO BETRAY THEIR KING! GUARDS! TAKE THEM AWAY—EXECUTE THEM.

Underground Attack

FROM II SAMUEL 5: 5-9

67

SURPRISED BY THE SUDDEN APPEARANCE OF DAVID'S MEN, THE GUARDS ARE QUICKLY OVERCOME.

GIVE THE ORDER TO OPEN THE GATES— OR DIE!

THE TERRIFIED OFFICER SHOUTS THE ORDER. THE HUGE GATES SWING OPEN...

AND DAVID'S ARMY CHARGES THROUGH...

68

The Enemy's Plot

WHEN THE HUGE GATES OF JERUSALEM SWING OPEN, DAVID'S ARMY RUSHES IN TO TAKE THE CITY. THE BATTLE IS SWIFT—AND THE PEOPLE WHO BOASTED THAT THE BLIND AND LAME COULD HOLD THE CITY QUICKLY SURRENDER.

I WILL MAKE THIS CITY MY CAPITAL. OBEY MY ORDERS AND YOU MAY LIVE HERE IN PEACE.

THE NEWS OF DAVID'S VICTORY TRAVELS FAST—IN THE PHILISTINE COURT, THE MESSAGE STIRS UP ACTION.

DAVID HAS BEEN MADE KING OF **ALL** ISRAEL, AND NOW HE HAS TAKEN JERUSALEM.

HE MUST BE STOPPED— AT ONCE!

THE SIGNAL IS GIVEN—AND DAVID'S MEN STORM THE PHILISTINE CAMP. BEFORE THIS SUDDEN DRIVE, THE ENEMY BREAKS AND RUNS—LEAVING THE STATUES OF THEIR GODS BEHIND THEM.

DAVID TAKES THE IDOLS AS TROPHIES OF WAR.

BURN EVERY IDOL! LEAVE NO TRACE OF THEIR EVIL INFLUENCE.

BUT WHILE DAVID'S SOLDIERS RETURN VICTORIOUS TO JERUSALEM, THE DEFEATED PHILISTINES PLOT THEIR REVENGE...

LET'S REORGANIZE OUR FORCES AND GO BACK TO THE VALLEY. THIS TIME _WE'LL_ MAKE THE SURPRISE ATTACK!

I CAN'T WAIT TO SEE DAVID ON HIS KNEES— BEGGING FOR MERCY!

The Mighty City

FROM II SAMUEL 5: 22-25; 5: 10, 11

BEFORE MAKING ANY MOVE AGAINST THE ENEMY, DAVID AGAIN SEEKS GOD'S HELP. GOD GIVES HIM TWO ORDERS...

FOLLOWING GOD'S DIRECTION, DAVID LEADS HIS ARMY IN A LARGE *SEMICIRCLE* UNTIL IT COMES UP *BEHIND* THE ENEMY CAMP. THEN HE WAITS FOR THE SECOND SIGN...

SUDDENLY THEY HEAR A SOUND IN THE TREETOPS— AS OF A MIGHTY ARMY ON THE MARCH.

IT IS THE SIGN—FROM GOD. ATTACK!

OBEDIENT TO GOD, DAVID ATTACKS FROM THE REAR AND DRIVES THE PHILISTINES OUT OF ISRAEL. THE KINGS OF NEIGHBORING COUNTRIES REALIZE THEY CANNOT DEFEAT DAVID— AND AGREE TO LIVE IN PEACE.

FREED FROM FEAR OF ATTACK, DAVID BEGINS BUILDING UP HIS CAPITAL CITY.

KING HIRAM OF TYRE SENT THOSE CEDAR LOGS—AND HIS OWN CARPENTERS TO HELP OUR BUILDERS.

WORK BEGINS ON A BEAUTIFUL PALACE FOR DAVID...

AND THE CITY WALLS ARE RE-ENFORCED.

THIS CITY IS SO STRONG THAT NO ONE WOULD DARE TO ATTACK IT.

THERE IS ONE THING MISSING, JOAB, IF WE ARE TO MAKE JERUSALEM TRULY STRONG!

74

God's Promises to David

FROM II SAMUEL 6, 7, 8, 9: 5; I CHRONICLES 13, 15, 16

JERUSALEM, THE CAPITAL OF ISRAEL, IS NOW A WELL-FORTIFIED CITY. BUT KING DAVID KNOWS THAT HIS NATION LACKS ONE THING TO MAKE IT SPIRITUALLY STRONG— A WAY FOR ISRAEL TO WORSHIP THE LORD. HE CALLS ON THE PEOPLE TO GO WITH HIM TO BRING GOD'S HOLY ARK TO JERUSALEM.

FATHER, WHAT'S IN THE GOLDEN CHEST?

TWO STONE TABLETS ON WHICH GOD'S TEN COMMANDMENTS ARE WRITTEN.

WHERE HAS IT BEEN?

THE PHILISTINES CAPTURED IT—BUT WHEN TROUBLE CAME TO THEM, THEY WERE AFRAID AND SENT IT BACK. IT HAS BEEN STORED AWAY FOR MANY YEARS.

THE ARK IS A SYMBOL OF GOD'S PRESENCE—SO IT IS A SACRED MOMENT FOR THE ISRAELITES WHEN THE ARK IS BROUGHT TO JERUSALEM.

WHO IS THIS KING OF GLORY?

LIFT UP YOUR HEADS, O YE GATES...AND THE KING OF GLORY SHALL COME IN!

THE LORD IS THE KING OF GLORY!

AS THE ARK IS PLACED IN ITS SPECIAL TENT, MUSICIANS APPOINTED BY DAVID BURST FORTH IN SONG.

GIVE UNTO THE LORD THE GLORY DUE UNTO HIS NAME: BRING AN OFFERING, AND COME BEFORE HIM: WORSHIP THE LORD IN THE BEAUTY OF HOLINESS.

BUT ONE DAY DAVID LOOKS AT THE TENT AND CALLS NATHAN, THE PROPHET OF GOD, TO HIM.

IT ISN'T RIGHT FOR GOD'S HOUSE TO BE A TENT WHILE I LIVE IN A PALACE. I'D LIKE TO BUILD A TEMPLE TO GOD.

I'M SURE GOD WOULD BE PLEASED.

THAT NIGHT GOD SPEAKS TO NATHAN—AND THE NEXT DAY NATHAN TELLS DAVID THAT GOD DOES NOT WANT HIM TO BUILD THE TEMPLE. BUT GOD PROMISES TO GIVE DAVID A SON WHO WILL BUILD A HOUSE FOR GOD—AND THAT HIS ROYAL LINE WILL LAST FOREVER. THIS SECOND PROMISE WAS FULFILLED IN JESUS, WHO WAS BORN OF THE ROYAL LINE OF DAVID AND REIGNS FOREVER.

THEN DAVID REMEMBERS A PROMISE HE HIMSELF MADE YEARS BEFORE TO HIS BEST FRIEND, JONATHAN. EACH HAD VOWED TO BE KIND TO THE OTHER'S CHILDREN. DAVID INQUIRES ABOUT JONATHAN'S FAMILY.

YES, PRINCE JONATHAN HAD A SON, MEPHIBOSHETH.

SEND FOR HIM.

REMEMBER, HE IS ALSO KING SAUL'S GRANDSON. BUT FOR YOU HE MIGHT BE SITTING ON THE THRONE OF ISRAEL. HE MAY HATE YOU...

77

A King Is Tempted

FROM II SAMUEL 9: 6—11: 14

"I WAS ONLY FIVE WHEN THE NEWS OF MY FATHER'S DEATH CAME. AS MY NURSE RAN IN FRIGHT, SHE DROPPED ME. I HAVE BEEN CRIPPLED EVER SINCE."

"I AM SORRY--AND I REGRET THAT YOUR GRANDFATHER'S LAND WAS NOT RESTORED TO YOU BEFORE. IT IS NOW YOURS--AND I INVITE YOU TO EAT EVERY DAY AT MY TABLE."

"I AM GRATEFUL FOR YOUR KINDNESS."

"AND I THANK GOD I AM ABLE TO KEEP MY PROMISE TO YOUR FATHER."

UNDER DAVID'S LEADERSHIP, ISRAEL GROWS STRONGER EVERY DAY. BUT RULERS OF THE COUNTRIES AROUND GROW WORRIED.

"WORD HAS COME THAT THE SYRIANS AND AMMONITES ARE JOINING FORCES AGAINST US."

"I CAN'T LEAVE JERUSALEM NOW, JOAB. CALL UP THE ARMY AND GO OUT TO MEET THEM."

JOAB TAKES CHARGE OF THE WAR. ABOUT A YEAR LATER, AS DAVID STROLLS ON THE ROOF OF HIS PALACE...

"WHO IS THAT BEAUTIFUL WOMAN?"

"BATH-SHEBA, THE WIFE OF URIAH, A SOLDIER IN YOUR ARMY."

DAVID SENDS A MESSENGER TO BRING BATH-SHEBA TO HIS COURT.

YOU SENT FOR ME, O KING?

SHE IS EVEN MORE BEAUTIFUL THAN I THOUGHT!

IF ONLY I COULD MARRY HER! THE PROBLEM IS, URIAH IS HER HUSBAND!

BUT SOLDIERS SOMETIMES DIE IN BATTLE. THAT'S IT!

THINKING ONLY OF HIS LOVE FOR BATH-SHEBA, DAVID SENDS FOR URIAH ON THE EXCUSE OF ASKING ABOUT THE WAR.

THE ENEMY IS STRONG. BUT JOAB THINKS WE CAN FORCE THEIR SURRENDER SOON.

I AM SURE OF IT. PREPARE TO RETURN TO THE FRONT--AND TAKE THIS MESSAGE TO JOAB.

80

King David's Sin

URIAH, THE HUSBAND OF BATH-SHEBA, RETURNS TO THE BATTLEFRONT WITH A MESSAGE FROM KING DAVID TO JOAB, GENERAL OF THE ISRAELITE FORCES

..., AND SENDS WORD TO DAVID.

WE FOUGHT BRAVELY-- BUT THE ARCHERS ON THE CITY WALLS HAD THE ADVANTAGE. URIAH, THE LEADER OF THE ATTACK, WAS KILLED.

TELL JOAB NOT TO FEEL BADLY-- WAR ALWAYS TAKES SOME OF OUR BEST MEN. STEP UP THE ATTACK AND TAKE THE CITY.

ACROSS THE CITY, BATH-SHEBA MOURNS FOR HER HUSBAND-- BUT IN HER HEART SHE KNOWS THAT NOW SHE IS FREE TO MARRY THE KING.

WHEN BATH-SHEBA'S TIME OF MOURNING IS OVER, DAVID CALLS HER TO THE PALACE, AND THEY ARE MARRIED.

LONG LIVE THE KING! LONG LIVE THE QUEEN!

LATER, WHEN A SON IS BORN TO BATH-SHEBA, THE KING AND ALL ISRAEL REJOICE... BUT GOD IS NOT PLEASED! EVEN WHILE THE PEOPLE SHOUT THEIR PRAISES, A MAN OF GOD IS ON HIS WAY TO THE PALACE....

The King's Punishment

FROM II SAMUEL 12: 1-14

DAVID HAS MARRIED THE BEAUTIFUL BATH-SHEBA. WHEN THEIR SON IS BORN, DAVID IS PROUD AND HAPPY. UNTIL ONE DAY... NATHAN, THE PROPHET OF GOD, COMES TO SEE HIM.

WELCOME, NATHAN. WHAT CAN I DO FOR YOU?

I HAVE COME TO TELL YOU ABOUT A GREAT INJUSTICE THAT HAS BEEN DONE IN YOUR KINGDOM.

INJUSTICE IN **MY** KINGDOM? TELL ME ABOUT IT.

THERE WERE TWO MEN IN A CITY...

ONE WAS RICH, THE OTHER POOR. THE RICH MAN HAD MANY FLOCKS, BUT THE POOR MAN HAD ONLY ONE LITTLE LAMB WHICH HE LOVED DEARLY.

ONE DAY THE RICH MAN HAD A GUEST. HE TOOK THE LAMB FROM THE POOR MAN AND HAD IT KILLED TO SERVE FOR THE FEAST.

DURING THE TELLING OF THE STORY DAVID'S ANGER MOUNTS...

A MAN WHO WOULD DO THAT SHOULD BE PUT TO DEATH!

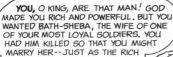

YOU, O KING, ARE THAT MAN! GOD MADE YOU RICH AND POWERFUL. BUT YOU WANTED BATH-SHEBA, THE WIFE OF ONE OF YOUR MOST LOYAL SOLDIERS. YOU HAD HIM KILLED SO THAT YOU MIGHT MARRY HER-- JUST AS THE RICH MAN TOOK THE POOR MAN'S LAMB!

I HAVE SINNED! I HAVE SINNED AGAINST THE LORD!

AND YOUR SIN WILL BRING TROUBLE TO YOU AND YOUR FAMILY. THE CHILD WHICH HAS BEEN BORN TO YOU AND BATH-SHEBA WILL DIE!

NO, NATHAN! NOT MY CHILD!

HE'S GONE!

Flight of the Brothers

FROM II SAMUEL 12: 15—13: 29

BOLDLY THE PROPHET NATHAN CHARGES KING DAVID WITH SINNING AGAINST THE LORD, AND FORETELLS THE DEATH OF DAVID'S YOUNGEST SON. WHEN NATHAN LEAVES, DAVID IS ALONE IN HIS SHAME. HE IS TRULY SORRY FOR THE CRIME HE HAS COMMITTED, AND TURNS TO GOD IN PRAYER...

CREATE IN ME A CLEAN HEART, O GOD; AND RENEW A RIGHT SPIRIT WITHIN ME.

THE SAME DAY WORD COMES THAT THE KING'S INFANT SON IS ILL...AND DAVID RUSHES TO THE SICKROOM.

HOW IS HE?

THERE IS LITTLE HOPE.

DAVID IS SICK WITH SORROW. HE FASTS AND PRAYS... BUT ON THE SEVENTH DAY HIS CHILD DIES.

MEANWHILE JOAB, DAVID'S GENERAL, CONTINUES THE SIEGE AGAINST THE CITY OF RABBAH. TO HONOR DAVID, HE SENDS WORD FOR THE KING TO COME AND MAKE THE FINAL ATTACK. DAVID LEADS THE CHARGE -- AND THE CITY SURRENDERS.

RETURNING VICTORIOUS INTO JERUSALEM, DAVID IS GREETED WITH SHOUTS OF PRAISE. HE IS PLEASED AND PROUD -- ISRAEL IS STRONG, AND NO NATION WOULD DARE ATTACK IT, BUT...

DAVID DOES NOT REALIZE THAT TROUBLE BUILDING UP WITHIN HIS OWN PALACE WALLS WILL ENDANGER HIS THRONE.

SOON AFTER DAVID'S TRIUMPHAL RETURN, PRINCE ABSALOM MAKES A SPECIAL VISIT TO HIS FATHER.

IT'S SHEEPSHEARING TIME, AND I'M HAVING A BIG FEAST IN THE COUNTRY. WILL YOU HONOR MY GUESTS WITH YOUR PRESENCE?

THANK YOU, ABSALOM, BUT IF YOU ARE HAVING A BIG FEAST, I DON'T WANT TO ADD TO YOUR EXPENSES.

THEN MAY MY BROTHERS COME? PRINCE AMNON CAN REPRESENT YOU.

AMNON? I THOUGHT ABSALOM HATED HIM.

YES, I'M PLEASED THAT YOU WANT TO HONOR YOUR BROTHERS THIS WAY.

ABSALOM DOES HATE HIS OLDER HALF-BROTHER, AMNON, WHO HAS FIRST RIGHT TO DAVID'S THRONE. WHEN AMNON ACCEPTS THE INVITATION, ABSALOM CALLS IN HIS SERVANTS.

AMNON IS COMING TO THE FEAST. WHEN I GIVE THE WORD--- KILL HIM!

AT THE HEIGHT OF THE FEAST, AMNON IS KILLED... AFRAID FOR THEIR LIVES, THE REST OF THE BROTHERS FLEE INTO THE NIGHT...

89

A Prince's Command!

FROM II SAMUEL 13: 30—14: 30

MESSENGERS BRING WORD TO THE PALACE IN JERUSALEM THAT KING, DAVID'S SON, ABSALOM, HAS KILLED ALL OF HIS BROTHERS. STUNNED BY SHOCK AND GRIEF, DAVID FALLS TO THE GROUND--WEEPING. BUT HIGH ON THE CITY WALLS THE MAN IN THE TOWER KEEPS WATCH...

LOOK! A BAND OF MEN RIDING THIS WAY!

THE MEN ARE DAVID'S SONS AND THEIR SERVANTS.

91

HE HASN'T ENTIRELY FORGIVEN YOU, ABSALOM. HE SAYS YOU CAN'T LIVE IN THE PALACE OR COME TO SEE HIM.

IF THAT'S THE WAY HE WANTS IT, ALL RIGHT.

HE WON[...] TREAT M[...] THIS W[...] FOR LON[...]

FOR TWO YEARS ABSALOM LIVES IN JERUSALEM WITHOUT SEEING HIS FATHER. HE RESENTS THIS TREATMENT AND HIS ANGER GROWS UNTIL AT LAST HE CAN STAND IT NO LONGER. HE SENDS FOR JOAB. JOAB REFUSES TO COME. ABSALOM SENDS A SECOND TIME.

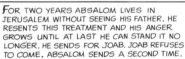

JOAB STILL WON'T COME, SIR.

OH, YES HE WILL-- AND IN A HURRY!

JOAB HAS A BARLEY FIELD NEXT TO MINE. SET FIRE TO IT!

92

Treason?

FROM II SAMUEL 14: 31—15: 4

WHEN DAVID'S GENERAL, JOAB, REFUSES TO OBEY PRINCE ABSALOM'S REQUEST TO COME TO HIM, ABSALOM ORDERS JOAB'S GRAINFIELD SET ON FIRE. AT THE SIGHT OF THE BURNING FIELD JOAB SETS OUT AT ONCE FOR ABSALOM'S HOUSE...

HE MAY BE A PRINCE--BUT SOME DAY I'LL GET EVEN WITH HIM FOR THIS.

YOUR SERVANTS SET FIRE TO MY GRAIN. WHY?

I SENT FOR YOU-- AND YOU REFUSED TO COME. I THOUGHT **THIS** WOULD BRING YOU.

93

I'M A PRINCE, AND I SHOULD BE TREATED LIKE MY BROTHERS. GO TO MY FATHER AND ASK HIM IF HE WILL SEE ME.

BUT...

HE ASKED ME TO COME BACK TO JERUSALEM. IF HE WANTS TO PUNISH ME FOR WHAT I DID LET HIM DO IT. IF NOT, THEN LET HIM TREAT ME LIKE A SON AGAIN.

JOAB CARRIES ABSALOM'S MESSAGE TO KING DAVID.

YOUR SON MISSES YOU— HE WISHES TO BE FORGIVEN AND WELCOMED BACK INTO THE FAMILY.

HE MISSES ME? NO MORE THAN I MISS HIM. TELL HIM TO COME TO ME.

ABSALOM PRETENDS TO BE HUMBLE AS HE BOWS BEFORE HIS FATHER--ASKING FORGIVENESS. BUT IN HIS HEART HE HAS AN EVIL PLAN.

RISE UP, ABSALOM. YOU ARE FORGIVEN. FROM NOW ON YOU WILL BE WELCOME AT THE PALACE AS A PRINCE OF ISRAEL.

95

Revolt!

FROM II SAMUEL 15: 7-13

FOR SEVERAL YEARS ABSALOM CARRIES ON A CAMPAIGN TO GAIN FOLLOWERS SO THAT HE CAN OVERTHROW HIS FATHER'S KINGDOM. AT LAST THE TIME IS RIPE FOR HIS FINAL MOVE... HE GOES TO HIS FATHER...

AFTER I KILLED MY BROTHER AND WAS LIVING IN GESHUR, I MADE A VOW THAT IF I COULD RETURN AGAIN TO JERUSALEM, I WOULD SERVE THE LORD. MAY I GO TO MY BIRTHPLACE, HEBRON, TO OFFER A SACRIFICE TO GOD?

YOU HAVE MY PERMISSION, SON, AND MY BLESSING.

ABSALOM GETS READY TO GO, BUT BEFORE HE LEAVES THE CITY...

GO TO ALL THE TRIBES OF ISRAEL-- INVITE THEM TO COME TO HEBRON. TELL THEM THAT WHEN THEY HEAR THE TRUMPET THEY ARE TO SHOUT: "ABSALOM IS THE RULER IN HEBRON!"

IN HEBRON ABSALOM WAITS UNTIL GREAT THRONGS OF HIS FOLLOWERS REACH THE CITY, THEN HE APPEARS BEFORE THE PEOPLE... THE TRUMPET SOUNDS...

ABSALOM! LONG LIVE THE KING!

ABSALOM IS THE RULER IN HEBRON.

LATER ABSALOM CALLS FOR AHITHOPHEL, HIS FATHER'S CHIEF ADVISER.

THINGS ARE GOING AS I HAVE PLANNED.

GOOD. IF KING DAVID TRIES TO FIGHT BACK, HE WON'T HAVE A CHANCE -- WITH **ME** TO ADVISE YOU!

97

98

Council of War

FROM II SAMUEL 15: 13—17: 13

THE NEWS THAT HIS OWN SON, ABSALOM, HAS LED A REVOLT AGAINST HIM LEAVES DAVID IN A STATE OF SHOCK.

ABSALOM! HOW CAN I FIGHT MY OWN SON--MY OWN PEOPLE? WHOM CAN I COUNT ON TO STAND WITH ME?

YOUR FRIENDS WILL MAKE THEMSELVES KNOWN.

WE MUST ESCAPE BEFORE ABSALOM ATTACKS THE CITY! TELL MY FAMILY-- MY SERVANTS -- ALL WHO ARE LOYAL--TO GET READY TO LEAVE JERUSALEM!

AT DAWN DAVID LEADS HIS PEOPLE OUT OF THE CITY--AT THE LAST HOUSE HE STOPS TO WATCH HIS FOLLOWERS PASS BY.

IN THE PROCESSION ARE THE PRIESTS CARRYING GOD'S HOLY ARK.

STOP--TAKE IT BACK TO THE CITY. IF GOD WILLS IT, I WILL RETURN TO THE CITY AND WORSHIP AGAIN BEFORE HIS ARK.

THE NUMBER WHO CHOOSE TO JOIN DAVID GROWS WITH EACH PASSING HOUR. BUT DAVID SENDS ONE OF THEM BACK...

HUSHAI, YOU CAN SERVE ME BETTER IF YOU OFFER TO HELP ABSALOM. MAYBE YOU CAN KEEP HIM FROM FOLLOWING THE ADVICE OF THOSE WHO HAVE BETRAYED ME.

YOU ARE MY KING, AND I WILL SERVE IN ANY WAY YOU ASK.

HUSHAI RETURNS -- IN TIME TO SEE ABSALOM RIDE INTO THE CITY. IN THE CROWDS THERE ARE SHOUTS OF JOY AND PRAISE -- BUT THERE IS ALSO FEAR...

THIS MEANS WAR!

LIKE THE MAN IN THE CROWD, HUSHAI KNOWS THAT WAR WILL SOON BE UPON THEM. HE OFFERS HIS SERVICES TO ABSALOM -- AND ALONG WITH AHITHOPHEL IS CALLED TO THE FIRST COUNCIL OF WAR. AHITHOPHEL SPEAKS FIRST.

WE MUST ATTACK WHILE DAVID IS WEAK AND ON THE RUN.

NO, AHITHOPHEL'S ADVICE IS NOT GOOD. DAVID AND HIS MEN ARE ISRAEL'S BEST FIGHTERS. AND RIGHT NOW THEY ARE ANGRY AS BEARS ROBBED OF THEIR YOUNG. IF YOU ATTACK AND SUFFER ANY DEFEAT, THE PEOPLE WILL TURN AGAINST YOU. WAIT UNTIL YOU CAN CALL UP THOUSANDS OF MEN... THEN IF YOU, O KING, LEAD THEM...

Hide-out in a Well

FROM II SAMUEL 17: 14-23

AHITHOPHEL HAS ADVISED ABSALOM TO ATTACK KING DAVID WHILE HE IS FLEEING FOR HIS LIFE. BUT HUSHAI—SECRETLY WORKING FOR DAVID—TELLS ABSALOM TO WAIT UNTIL HIS OWN FORCES ARE BETTER PREPARED.

NO! NO! HUSHAI'S ADVICE WILL HELP YOUR FATHER MORE THAN YOU. GIVE DAVID TIME TO GET **HIS** FORCES PREPARED, AND THE BATTLE IS HIS. REMEMBER—DEFEAT MEANS DEATH TO ALL OF US!

BUT ABSALOM WILL NOT LISTEN. AHITHOPHEL IS **SO** SURE THE REBELLION WILL FAIL—AND HE WILL DIE A TRAITOR'S DEATH—THAT HE GOES HOME AND COMMITS SUICIDE.

MEANWHILE, BACK IN JERUSALEM, HUSHAI'S WELL-ORGANIZED PLAN IS BEING CARRIED OUT.

TWO OF OUR MEN ARE WAITING AT THE KIDRON FOUNTAIN. TELL THEM WHAT WE HAVE TOLD YOU. BE CAREFUL—KING DAVID'S LIFE IS IN YOUR HANDS!

WITH A WATER JUG ON HER HEAD, THE GIRL WALKS BOLDLY OUT OF THE CITY GATE...

AND AT THE APPOINTED PLACE MEETS THE TWO MEN.

TELL KING DAVID NOT TO STOP UNTIL HE HAS REACHED THE OTHER SIDE OF THE JORDAN RIVER.

THE MEN LEAVE, BUT ON THE WAY...

DON'T LOOK NOW, BUT I THINK WE HAVE BEEN SEEN. LET'S PLAY IT SAFE AND HIDE OUT IN BAHURIM.

SPIES!

THE BOY RACES BACK TO THE CITY AND REPORTS WHAT HE HAS SEEN TO PRINCE ABSALOM.

FIND THOSE SPIES AND BRING THEM TO ME!

ABSALOM'S SOLDIERS FOLLOW THE TRAIL UNTIL THEY REACH A HOUSE IN BAHURIM...

WE'RE SEARCHING FOR SPIES... HAS ANYONE BEEN HERE?

YES, TWO MEN. BUT THEY LEFT-- IN THE DIRECTION OF THE RIVER.

THE SOLDIERS SEARCH THE HOUSE, BUT WHEN THEY FIND NOTHING, THEY MOVE ON.

COME UP-- THE SOLDIERS HAVE GONE.

EVEN ABSALOM'S MEN WOULDN'T KNOW THERE WAS A WELL HERE. I'M GLAD IT WAS A DRY ONE.

I'M PROUD TO HELP MY KING, BUT-- GO-- THE SOLDIERS MIGHT RETURN.

THE MESSENGERS HURRY ON... AND THAT NIGHT DAVID AND HIS FOLLOWERS CROSS OVER THE JORDAN.

104

her Against Son

BSALOM'S SOLDIERS SEARCH THE MESSENGERS WHO HAVE EN SENT TO WARN DAVID. WHEN EY CANNOT FIND THEM, THEY RETURN JERUSALEM. MEANWHILE, DAVID D HIS FOLLOWERS REACH THE Y OF MAHANAIM.

HERE'S SOME FOOD AND BEDDING MY MASTER HAS SENT FOR KING DAVID AND HIS FRIENDS.

GOD BLESS YOU. TELL YOUR MASTER I WILL NOT FORGET HIS KINDNESS.

AVID QUICKLY ORGANIZES HIS ARMY AND WAITS OR THE MESSAGE HE EXPECTS — BUT DREADS.

PRINCE ABSALOM AND HIS FORCES HAVE CROSSED THE JORDAN RIVER!

106

THE ARMIES MEET HEAD-ON IN THE WOODS OF EPHRAIM. DAVID'S MEN ATTACK WITH SUCH FURY THAT ABSALOM'S ARMY IS THROWN INTO PANIC ... AND RETREATS.

THE BATTLE IS LOST. ABSALOM IS AFRAID THAT IF HE IS CAUGHT HE WILL SUFFER A TRAITOR'S DEATH. HE TRIES TO ESCAPE...

AND IS CAUGHT IN THE LOW-HANGING BRANCH OF AN OAK!

PRINCE ABSALOM'S REVOLT AGAINST HIS FATHER, KING DAVID, LEADS TO A TERRIBLE BATTLE IN THE WOODS OF EPHRAIM. WHEN ABSALOM SEES THAT THE FIGHT IS GOING AGAINST HIM, HE TRIES TO ESCAPE, BUT...

GENERAL JOAB! ABSALOM IS CAUGHT-- BACK THERE-- IN A TREE!

ABSALOM? WHY DIDN'T YOU KILL HIM ON THE SPOT!

ILL THE KING'S SON? EVER! I HEARD DAVID ELL YOU AND THE THER LEADERS TO E CAREFUL OF ABSALOM.

WE'RE WASTING TIME-- I'LL DO IT MYSELF!

MESSENGERS CARRY NEWS OF THE BATTLE TO DAVID.

MY SON, ABSALOM. IS HE ALL RIGHT?

MAY ALL THE KING'S ENEMIES BE AS THAT YOUNG MAN!

JOAB AND HIS ARMOR-BEARERS RUSH BACK TO THE TREE AND KILL ABSALOM. THE TRUMPET OF VICTORY IS SOUNDED-- THE BATTLE IS OVER!

ROKENHEARTED, DAVID CLIMBS THE LOOKOUT ABOVE THE GATE. ONE, HE MOURNS FOR HIS SON.

MY SON SALOM. OULD I HAD ED INSTEAD YOU. MY N! MY SON!

IN HIS GRIEF DAVID TURNS HIS BACK ON THE MEN WHO WON THE VICTORY FOR HIM. FINALLY JOAB GOES TO SEE THE KING.

YOU ACT AS IF YOU WISH ABSALOM HAD WON THE VICTORY! HAVE YOU FORGOTTEN THE MEN WHO FOUGHT TO SAVE YOU-- YOUR FAMILY--AND YOUR KINGDOM? IF THIS KEEPS UP, ALL YOUR FRIENDS WILL TURN AGAINST YOU!

DAVID SEES THE TRUTH OF JOAB'S WORDS. HE MAKES PEACE WITH THE TRIBES THAT HAD SIDED WITH ABSALOM... AND GOES BACK TO JERUSALEM.

SOON AFTER THE ROYAL FAMILY IS SETTLED AGAIN IN THE PALACE, QUEEN BATH-SHEBA SPEAKS TO DAVID.

WHEN OUR SON, SOLOMON, WAS BORN, YOU PROMISED THAT HE WOULD BE KING AFTER YOU. BUT I FEAR HIS HALF-BROTHERS WILL CAUSE TROUBLE.

HAVE NO FEAR. SOLOMON WILL RULE ISRAEL.

YEARS PASS -- AND DAVID GROWS OLD. FINALLY WORD SPREADS THROUGHOUT JERUSALEM THAT THE KING'S HEALTH IS FAILING FAST. THE PEOPLE KNOW THAT DAVID HAS CHOSEN SOLOMON TO BE KING AND TO BUILD THE TEMPLE OF GOD. BUT THERE ARE RUMORS...

AND IN THE PALACE, ONE OF DAVID'S SONS, ADONIJAH, MEETS WITH THE HIGH PRIEST, ABIATHAR, AND GENERAL JOAB.

MY FATHER IS GROWING WEAKER -- AND THE TIME HAS COME FOR ME TO CARRY OUT OUR PLAN. BRING ALL THE KING'S SONS -- EXCEPT MY HALF-BROTHER SOLOMON -- AND MEET ME AT THE SERPENT STONE.

110

he Plot that Failed

KING DAVID IS GROWING WEAKER... HIS OLDEST SON, ADONIJAH, KNOWS THAT IF HE IS TO ACCOMPLISH HIS PURPOSE, HE MUST ACT SWIFTLY. SECRETLY HE INVITES SOME OF HIS FRIENDS TO A FEAST OUTSIDE THE CITY... AND PROCLAIMS HIMSELF KING.

EAT AND BE MERRY — BEFORE THIS DAY IS OVER I WILL SIT ON THE THRONE OF ISRAEL. AND YOU, MY FRIENDS, WILL BE REWARDED FOR YOUR LOYALTY.

THE BOOKS, 1 AND 2 KINGS AND 2 CHRONICLES, RECORD THE HISTORY OF THE HEBREW EMPIRE THROUGH THE YEARS OF SOLOMON'S REIGN, THE DIVISION OF THE KINGDOM INTO TWO SEPARATE NATIONS, JUDAH AND ISRAEL-- AND THE FALL OF BOTH.

BUT WHILE ADONIJAH IS FEASTING, NATHAN, THE PROPHET OF GOD, IS TALKING WITH QUEEN BATH-SHEBA.

HAVE YOU HEARD--ADONIJAH HAS PROCLAIMED HIMSELF KING! IF YOU WOULD SAVE YOURSELF AND YOUR SON, SOLOMON, DO AS I SAY.

TELL ME-- AND I'LL DO IT.

As SOLOMON RETURNS TO THE CITY, THE PEOPLE GREET THEIR NEW KING WITH SHOUTS OF JOY.

SO GREAT IS THE NOISE OF THE CELEBRATION THAT IT REACHES ADONIJAH'S FEAST.

WHAT'S GOING ON IN THE CITY?

AT THAT MOMENT A MESSENGER ENTERS...

WHAT GOOD NEWS DO YOU HAVE FOR US?

THE NOISE YOU HEAR IS THE SHOUTING OF ALL JERUSALEM! DAVID HAS MADE SOLOMON KING.

KNOWING THAT THEY MAY BE BRANDED AS TRAITORS, ADONIJAH'S GUESTS FLEE IN TERROR.

THERE'S ONLY ONE CHANCE TO SAVE MY LIFE.

Death of a King
FROM I KINGS 1: 49—2: 46

WHEN PRINCE ADONIJAH LEARNS THAT HIS FATHER, KING DAVID, HAS MADE SOLOMON KING OF ALL ISRAEL, ADONIJAH KNOWS THAT HIS OWN PLOT TO STEAL THE THRONE HAS FAILED. IN FEAR FOR HIS LIFE, HE RUNS TO THE TABERNACLE AND GRABS HOLD OF THE HORNS ON THE ALTAR OF SACRIFICE.

I WILL NOT LET GO UNTIL SOLOMON PROMISES NOT TO KILL ME.

SOLOMON AGREES TO SPARE ADONIJAH'S LIFE **IF** HE PROVES HIMSELF WORTHY OF THE KING'S TRUST. ADONIJAH PROMISES AND IS BROUGHT BEFORE HIS YOUNG HALF-BROTHER.

MY LORD AND KING!

SOLOMON LATER BELIEVES BOTH ADONIJAH AND GENERAL JOAB TO BE DISLOYAL, AND THEY ARE EXECUTED.

ONE DAY DAVID CALLS SOLOMON TO HIM.

MY SON, I AM DYING. THIS IS MY LAST COUNSEL TO YOU: BE STRONG AND SHOW YOURSELF A MAN. KEEP GOD'S COMMANDMENTS AND WALK IN HIS WAYS...

AND IS BURIED IN A TOMB WITHIN THE WALLS OF JERUSALEM, THE CAPITAL OF HIS KINGDOM.

THEN DAVID, WHO RULED ISRAEL FOR FORTY YEARS, DIES...

ALL ISRAEL MOURNS THE DEATH OF THE SHEPHERD BOY WHO BUILT ISRAEL INTO A MIGHTY EMPIRE AND WHOSE FAITH IN GOD IS REVEALED IN ONE OF HIS PSALMS.

Psalm 23

The Lord is my shepherd; I shall not want. He maketh me to lie down in green pastures: He leadeth me beside the still waters. He restoreth my soul: He leadeth me in the paths of righteousness for his name's sake.

Yea, though I walk through the valley of the shadow of death, I will fear no evil: for thou art with me; Thy rod and thy staff they comfort me.

Thou preparest a table before me in the presence of mine enemies: Thou anointest my head with oil; My cup runneth over.

Surely goodness and mercy shall follow me all the days of my life: And I will dwell in the house of the Lord forever.

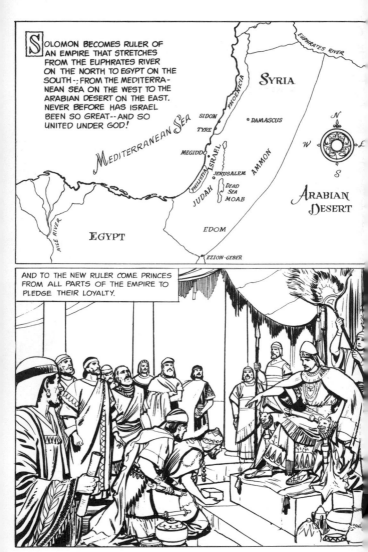

SOLOMON BECOMES RULER OF AN EMPIRE THAT STRETCHES FROM THE EUPHRATES RIVER ON THE NORTH TO EGYPT ON THE SOUTH-; FROM THE MEDITERRANEAN SEA ON THE WEST TO THE ARABIAN DESERT ON THE EAST. NEVER BEFORE HAS ISRAEL BEEN SO GREAT--AND SO UNITED UNDER GOD!

AND TO THE NEW RULER COME PRINCES FROM ALL PARTS OF THE EMPIRE TO PLEDGE THEIR LOYALTY.

116

God's Promise to a King

FROM I KINGS 3: 1-27

SOLOMON, THE NEW KING OF ISRAEL, LOVES GOD, AS DID HIS FATHER, DAVID, AND HE IS EAGER TO RULE HIS PEOPLE WELL. ONE DAY HE LEADS HIS PEOPLE TO THE ALTAR AT GIBEON TO WORSHIP GOD.

THAT NIGHT IN A DREAM SOLOMON HEARS GOD ASK HIM WHAT HE WANTS MOST IN LIFE. AND SOLOMON ANSWERS: "GIVE THY SERVANT AN UNDERSTANDING HEART TO JUDGE THY PEOPLE." GOD IS PLEASED, AND PROMISES NOT ONLY WISDOM, BUT RICHES, AND HONOR ABOVE ALL MEN.

118

119

The Golden Age

FROM I KINGS 3: 25—7: 51

ONE OF THE FIRST TESTS OF SOLOMON'S WISDOM COMES WHEN TWO WOMEN CLAIM THE SAME CHILD. SOLOMON ORDERS THE CHILD CUT IN TWO SO THAT EACH WOMAN MIGHT HAVE HALF. ONE WOMAN AGREES-- BUT THE OTHER CRIES OUT TO SAVE THE BABY EVEN IF SHE MUST GIVE HIM UP.

GIVE THE CHILD TO THE WOMAN WHO WOULD RATHER LOSE HIM THAN HAVE HIM KILLED. SHE IS THE MOTHER!

THE NEWS OF SOLOMON'S WISE DECISION SPREADS OVER ALL ISRAEL. SOON EVERYONE IS TALKING ABOUT THE YOUNG KING.

HE IS THE WISEST MAN WHO EVER LIVED.

SURELY GOD IS GUIDING SOLOMON. UNDER HIM, ISRAEL WILL BECOME EVEN GREATER THAN IT WAS UNDER DAVID.

THE PEOPLE ARE HAPPY. ISRAEL IS AT PEACE. SOLOMON ESTABLISHES GOOD RELATIONS WITH MANY OF THE NEIGHBORING COUNTRIES BY MARRYING PRINCESSES OF THOSE NATIONS. RULERS OF THE COUNTRIES CONQUERED BY DAVID PAY TRIBUTE MONEY TO SOLOMON'S TREASURY. SO BEGINS THE GOLDEN AGE OF ISRAEL.

...LAUNCH HIS FIRST GREAT ...ILDING PROJECT, SOLOMON ...NDS A MESSENGER TO HIS ...THER'S OLD FRIEND, KING ...AM OF TYRE.

KING SOLOMON SENDS HIS GREETINGS--AND ASKS IF YOU WILL SEND HIM CEDAR AND CYPRESS LOGS AND SKILLED WORKERS TO HELP HIM BUILD A TEMPLE TO GOD IN JERUSALEM.

...LESSED BE THE LORD FOR ...ING MY FRIEND DAVID SUCH ...WISE SON. TELL YOUR KING ...WILL GIVE HIM WHAT HE ASKS ...EXCHANGE FOR WHEAT AND OIL, WHICH ARE SCARCE IN OUR COUNTRY.

THE DEAL IS MADE--AND SOON MEN BY THE THOUSANDS ARE ORDERED TO WORK IN THE FORESTS OF LEBANON, CUTTING CEDAR TREES FOR SOLOMON'S TEMPLE.

ON THE SEACOAST WEST OF THE LEBANON FORESTS THE LOGS ARE TIED TOGETHER TO FORM GIANT RAFTS. THESE ARE FLOATED DOWN TO ISRAEL.

AT THE SEAPORT OF JOPPA THE LOG RAFTS ARE BROKEN UP, AND THE TIMBERS ARE DRAGGED MORE THAN THIRTY MILES ACROSS RUGGED COUNTRY TO JERUSAL...

NEAR JERUSALEM, THOUSANDS OF MEN TOIL IN THE GREAT QUARRIES.

CHISEL A BIT FROM THIS SIDE. EVERY STONE MUST BE MADE TO FIT PERFECTLY.

MEANWHILE, WOOD CARVERS AND GOLDBEATE... ARE AT WORK IN JERUSALEM.

THESE DOORS WOULD BE BEAUTIFUL JUST AS THEY ARE.

COVERED WITH GOLD, THE... BE THE FINEST... THE WORLD.

SLOWLY, CAREFULLY, FO... SEVEN LONG YEARS T... WORK GOES ON; UNT... AT LAST, THE MOST BE... TIFUL BUILDING IN ALL ISRAEL IS FINISHED...

e Temple of God

AFTER SEVEN LONG YEARS OF HARD WORK, THE MAGNIFICENT TEMPLE OF GOD IS COMPLETED. MEN, WOMEN, AND CHILDREN FROM ALL CORNERS OF ISRAEL CROWD INTO JERUSALEM TO WATCH THE PRIESTS CARRY THE SACRED ARK INTO THE TEMPLE. INSIDE, IN THE HOLY OF HOLIES-- DARK, WINDOWLESS, HEAVILY CURTAINED ROOM--THE ARK IS CAREFULLY PLACED BENEATH THE PROTECTING WINGS OF TWO FIFTEEN-FOOT GOLDEN CHERUBIM.

THEN, BEFORE ALL THE PEOPLE OF ISRAEL, SOLOMON KNEELS IN PRAYER.

O LORD, THERE IS NO GOD LIKE THEE! FORGIVE AND GUIDE THY PEOPLE AS THOU DIDST GUIDE MOSES WHO BROUGHT US OUT OF SLAVERY IN EGYPT.

BUT SOLOMON'S BUILDING PROGRAM DOES NOT END WITH THE TEMPLE. SOON A LARGE PALACE IS UNDER CONSTRUCTION.

O SOLOMON, IT WILL BE BEAUTIFUL. CEDAR-- BRONZE AND GOLD!

I MEA TO MA JERUSA THE MO BEAUTIF CITY IN T WORLD

AND RICHES KEEP POURING IN FROM MANY COUNTRIES. SHIPS FROM ARABIA AND AFRICA BRING RARE AND PRECIOUS GIFTS.

PEACOCKS --IVORY--OF WHAT USE ARE THEY?

WHEN YOU'RE AS RICH AS SOLOMON, THINGS DON'T HAVE TO BE USEFUL.

BUT NOT EVERYONE IN ISR IS RICH. OUTSIDE THE CIT JERUSALEM PEOPLE AR BEGINNING TO COMPLAI

THERE! THAT MY SHARE (GRAIN FOR KI SOLOMON'S HORSES.

A Queen's Visit

FROM I KINGS 10: 2—11: 8

THE FAME OF SOLOMON'S WEALTH AND WISDOM SPREADS FAR AND WIDE. IN THE ARABIAN PENINSULA, THE QUEEN OF SHEBA IS SO CURIOUS THAT SHE SETS OUT ON A TRIP TO JERUSALEM TO SEE FOR HERSELF WHETHER THE STORIES ARE TRUE.

INSIDE THE CITY, SHE IS EVEN MORE IMPRESSED WITH THE THRONE OF ISRAEL'S KING.

I HAVE HEARD SO MUCH OF YOUR WEALTH AND WISDOM THAT I HAD TO SEE YOU.

WELCOME, GRACIOUS QUEEN. ONCE I PRAYED TO GOD TO MAKE ME WISE. I HOPE YOU FIND THAT HE HAS.

SOLOMON ANSWERS ALL OF THE QUEEN'S QUESTIONS -- THEN HE TAKES HER FOR A TOUR OF THE CITY TO SEE THE BEAUTIFUL TEMPLE OF GOD - THE GIANT MARBLE PALACES - STABLES HOLDING THOUSANDS OF FINE HORSES.

128

The King Is Dead

FROM I KINGS 11: 29—12: 3

THERE IS TROUBLE IN ISRAEL. HIGH TAXES ANGER THE PEOPLE... SOME EVEN TALK OF REVOLT. BUT KING SOLOMON REFUSES TO HEED THE WARNING SIGNS. ONE DAY AS THE KING'S LABOR FOREMAN, JEROBOAM, LEAVES JERUSALEM...

JEROBOAM! STOP! I HAVE A MESSAGE FOR YOU FROM GOD.

AHIJAH!

A MESSAGE FROM GOD? WHAT IS IT? AND WHY ARE YOU TEARING YOUR ROBE?

THIS IS HOW SOLOMON'S KINGDOM WILL BE TORN APART-- BECAUSE HE HAS TURNED AWAY FROM GOD.

AHIJAH TEARS THE ROBE INTO TWELVE STRIPS.

HERE, TAKE THESE TEN PIECES. THEY REPRESENT THE TEN TRIBES OF ISRAEL OVER WHICH YOU WILL RULE WHEN SOLOMON DIES. THE OTHER TWO TRIBES WILL BE GIVEN TO SOLOMON'S SON.

SOLOMON FLIES INTO A RAGE WHEN HE LEARNS OF AHIJAH'S PROPHECY.

I MADE JEROBOAM A LEADER-- NOW HE IS USING HIS POSITION TO TURN PEOPLE AGAINST ME! FIND HIM AND KILL HIM!

BUT FRIENDS WARN JEROBOAM-- AND HE ESCAPES INTO EGYPT.

I'LL STAY HERE UNTIL SOLOMON DIES. THEN WE'LL SEE IF AHIJAH SPOKE THE TRUTH ABOUT MY RULING THE NORTHERN TRIBES OF ISRAEL.

REPORTS OF YOUR PEOPLE'S COMPLAINTS HAVE BEEN REACHING US FOR SOME TIME.

BUT SOLOMON CONTINUES TO LIVE IN LUXURY -- AND SO FAR REMOVED FROM HIS PEOPLE THAT THEIR COMPLAINTS DO NOT REACH HIM. HE EVEN IGNORES AHIJAH'S PROPHECY AND GOD'S WARNING THAT THE KINGDOM WILL BE DIVIDED BECAUSE HE WORSHIPS FALSE GODS.

AT LAST HE EVEN JOINS HIS FOREIGN WIVES IN THEIR WORSHIP OF HEATHEN IDOLS.

JUST TO PLEASE ME, PRAY TO MY GOD, SOLOMON.

IT CAN DO NO HARM--I STILL PRAY EVERY DAY TO THE GOD OF ISRAEL.

FIRST THE KING-- AND NOW THE PEOPLE WORSHIP HEATHEN IDOLS. NO COUNTRY THAT TURNS AWAY FROM GOD CAN REMAIN STRONG AND FREE. ISRAEL IS DOOMED.

THEN SOLOMON DIES! WITH GOD'S HELP HE HAD BUILT ISRAEL INTO A STRONG NATION. BUT IN HIS GREED FOR MORE WEALTH AND POWER HE HAD TURNED AWAY FROM GOD--AND HIS MIGHTY KINGDOM BEGINS TO CRUMBLE...

WHILE ISRAEL MOURNS THE DEATH OF ITS KING, A MESSENGER CARRIES THE NEWS OF HIS DEATH TO EGYPT.

JEROBOAM, I BRING NEWS! KING SOLOMON IS DEAD. HIS SON, REHOBOAM, HAS TAKEN HIS PLACE. THE PEOPLE WANT YOU TO COME HOME AND PRESENT THEIR CASE TO THE NEW KING.

I'LL GO AT ONCE!

The Kingdom Is Divided

FROM I KINGS 12: 4-27

SOLOMON IS DEAD! HIS SON, REHOBOAM, HAS GONE TO SHECHEM TO BE CROWNED KING OF ALL ISRAEL. WHEN JEROBOAM RETURNS FROM EXILE IN EGYPT, HE PLEADS FOR HIS PEOPLE.

YOUR FATHER FORCED US TO PAY HEAVY TAXES AND TO WORK HARD ON HIS BUILDING PROJECTS. WE CANNOT CONTINUE TO CARRY SUCH BURDENS. LIGHTEN OUR LOAD, AND WE WILL SERVE YOU, BUT...

COME BACK IN THREE DAYS AND I WILL GIVE YOU MY ANSWER.

REHOBOAM CONSULTS HIS ADVISERS. THE OLDER MEN TELL HIM TO HEED THE CRIES OF HIS PEOPLE, BUT HIS YOUNG FRIENDS...

NOW IS THE TIME TO LET THEM KNOW THAT YOU RULE WITH AN EVEN STRONGER HAND THAN YOUR FATHER.

THREE DAYS LATER THE PEOPLE RETURN FOR THE KING'S ANSWER.

MY FATHER MADE YOUR YOKE HEAVY. I'LL MAKE IT HEAVIER. MY FATHER BEAT YOU WITH LEATHER WHIPS. I'LL STING YOU WITH LEADED LASHES.

134

OUR BIBLE IN PICTURES
Idol Worship in Israel
FROM I KINGS 12:28—16:34

KING JEROBOAM RULES THE NORTHERN TRIBES, KNOWN AS ISRAEL, AND KING REHOBOAM RULES THE SOUTHERN KINGDOM OF JUDAH.

KING JEROBOAM IS AFRAID THAT IF HIS PEOPLE GO TO JERUSALEM TO WORSHIP IN THE TEMPLE, KING REHOBOAM WILL WIN THEM BACK TO HIS KINGDOM. TO PREVENT THIS, JEROBOAM MAKES TWO GOLDEN CALVES...

YEARS AGO WHEN OUR PEOPLE ESCAPED FROM EGYPT, THEY WORSHIPED THIS GOD. WORSHIP IT NOW AND YOU WILL NOT NEED TO MAKE THE LONG, HARD TRIP TO JERUSALEM.

HAVING GIVEN THE PEOPLE IDOLS TO WORSHIP, JEROBOAM FEELS THAT ALL IS WELL IN HIS KINGDOM, UNTIL ONE DAY...

OUR SON IS VERY ILL, JEROBOAM. I'M WORRIED.

SO AM I. IF ONLY I KNEW --BUT I KNOW SOMEONE WHO DOES--

135

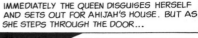

AHIJAH, THE PROPHET! HE TOLD ME I WOULD BE KING. HE KNOWS WHAT WILL HAPPEN. DISGUISE YOURSELF SO THAT HE WILL NOT KNOW YOU AND GO TO HIM.

IMMEDIATELY THE QUEEN DISGUISES HERSELF AND SETS OUT FOR AHIJAH'S HOUSE. BUT AS SHE STEPS THROUGH THE DOOR...

I AM BLIND--BUT I KNOW WHO YOU ARE AND WHY YOU HAVE COME! TELL YOUR HUSBAND, JEROBOAM, THAT HE HAS DONE EVIL--AND EVIL WILL COME TO HIM. HIS CHILD WILL DIE--AND ONE DAY THE PEOPLE OF ISRAEL WILL BE SCATTERED IN OTHER LANDS BECAUSE THEY HAVE WORSHIPED IDOLS.

THE FIRST PART OF AHIJAH'S PROPHECY COMES TRUE AT ONCE-- WHEN THE QUEEN RETURNS HOME SHE FINDS HER SON DEAD! BUT JEROBOAM IS NOT WISE ENOUGH TO HEED THIS WARNING. HE CONTINUES TO LEAD HIS PEOPLE IN IDOL WORSHIP, AND EVERY KING OF ISRAEL AFTER HIM FOLLOWS HIS EVIL PRACTICE. AT LAST KING AHAB COMES TO THE THRONE, AND...

ONE DAY A CARAVAN ENTERS SAMARIA, THE CAPITAL OF NORTHERN ISRAEL, WHERE KING AHAB HAS HIS PALACE.

THAT'S A RICH CARAVAN-- WONDER WHERE IT'S FROM AND WHO CAN AFFORD TO TRAVEL IN SUCH STYLE?

IT'S AHAB'S NEW WIFE-- JEZEBEL -- THE DAUGHTER OF THE HEATHEN KING OF TYRE.

137

SOON A STRANGE TEMPLE IS BUILT IN SAMARIA.

IT'S FINISHED, JEZEBEL, THE TEMPLE TO YOUR GOD, BAAL.

MY GOD? YOUR GOD, AHAB, AND EVERYBODY'S GOD. ONLY BAAL SHALL BE WORSHIPED WHERE I AM QUEEN.

THAT WON'T BE EASY --THERE ARE STILL PEOPLE IN ISRAEL WHO WORSHIP ISRAEL'S GOD.

THEY'LL WORS⌷ ISRAEL'S GO⌷ NO LONGER-- I HAVE ORDERED THEM PUT TO DEAT⌷

AND AS SUDDENLY AS HE APPEARED, THE STRANGER IS GONE!

WHO WAS THAT MAN? WHO LET HIM IN? WHY DID YOU LET HIM GET AWAY?

THAT WAS ELIJAH — A PROPHET OF ISRAEL'S GOD. HE IS A MAN OF MYSTERY — HE COMES AND GOES LIKE THE WIND.

A PROPHET OF GOD? FIND HIM AND PUT HIM TO DEATH INSTANTLY.

WHAT DID THAT CRAZY MAN SAY ABOUT NO RAIN OR DEW UNTIL HE CALLS FOR IT? NONSENSE! BAAL CONTROLS THE RAIN.

ELIJAH IS A PROPHET OF GOD. I WONDER...

AND AS THE MONTHS GO BY, AHAB CONTINUES TO WONDER...

EVERYTHING IS DRYING FROM LACK OF RAIN. MAYBE ELIJAH DID HAVE SOMETHING TO DO WITH THIS DROUGHT.

141

Miracle on a Rooftop

FROM I KINGS 17: 8—18: 8

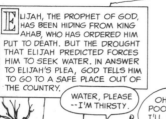

ELIJAH, THE PROPHET OF GOD, HAS BEEN HIDING FROM KING AHAB, WHO HAS ORDERED HIM PUT TO DEATH. BUT THE DROUGHT THAT ELIJAH PREDICTED FORCES HIM TO SEEK WATER. IN ANSWER TO ELIJAH'S PLEA, GOD TELLS HIM TO GO TO A SAFE PLACE OUT OF THE COUNTRY.

WATER, PLEASE --I'M THIRSTY.

OH, YOU POOR MAN. I'LL BRING YOU SOME RIGHT AWAY.

BUT WE HAVE ONLY A HANDFUL OF FLOUR AND A FEW DROPS OF OIL LEFT. WHEN THAT'S GONE-- I DON'T KNOW WHAT WE'LL DO.

DON'T WORRY. GOD HAS SENT ME HERE TO HIDE FROM KING AHAB. GOD WILL SEE THAT THERE IS ENOUGH FOOD FOR ALL OF US.

143

O LORD MY GOD, I PRAY THAT THIS CHILD'S SOUL MAY COME INTO HIM AGAIN.

GOD ANSWERS ELIJAH'S PRAYER, AND IN A MOMENT...

SEE, YOUR SON IS ALL RIGHT.

OH, THANK YOU--THANK YOU. NOW I KNOW THAT YOU ARE A MAN OF GOD

WHILE ELIJAH IS IN HIDING, KING AHAB BECOMES FRANTIC BECAUSE OF THE DROUGHT. HE FINALLY CALLS FOR OBADIAH, A MAN WHO HAS REMAINED TRUE TO GOD.

WE MUST FIND WATER--BEFORE ALL OF OUR ANIMALS DIE. YOU SEARCH IN ONE DIRECTION, AND I'LL SEARCH THE OTHER.

OBADIAH SETS OUT--AND ON THE WAY HE IS SURPRISED TO SEE ELIJAH COMING.

ELIJAH! IS IT REALLY YOU?

YES, GOD HAS SENT ME TO SEE KING AHAB. GO, TELL HIM I AM HERE.

hallenge on Mt. Carmel

OM I KINGS 18: 17-37

MONTHS GO BY AND STILL THERE IS NO RAIN IN ISRAEL. AT LAST KING AHAB HIMSELF IS FORCED TO SEARCH THE COUNTRY TO FIND PASTURES FOR HIS ANIMALS. MEANTIME GOD SENDS THE PROPHET, ELIJAH, TO SEE THE KING. THE TWO MEET.

ELIJAH! IS IT YOU -- THE ONE WHO HAS CAUSED US SO MUCH TROUBLE?

IT IS NOT **I** WHO BROUGHT DROUGHT TO ISRAEL, BUT YOU, O KING IT IS **YOU** WHO HAVE BROKEN GOD'S COMMANDMENTS AND WORSHIPED BAAL.

SEND FOR THE PROPHETS OF BAAL -- ALL 450 OF THEM -- AND THE LEADERS OF ISRAEL. THEN MEET ME ON MOUNT CARMEL.

AHAB IS SO AWED BY THE AUTHORITY WITH WHICH ELIJAH SPEAKS THAT HE DOES AS THE PROPHET COMMANDS. SOON A GREAT CROWD GATHERS ON TOP OF THE MOUNTAIN BY THE SEA.

145

146

THE PROPHETS OF BAAL ARE FORCED TO ACCEPT THE CHALLENGE. WITH GREAT CEREMONY THEY PREPARE THE SACRIFICE... AND BEGIN TO CHANT AND CALL UPON THEIR GOD.

AS THE HOURS PASS THEY SING LOUDER AND LOUDER.

CALL A LITTLE LOUDER-- PERHAPS BAAL IS TALKING --OR OFF ON A JOURNEY-- OR ASLEEP.

BY MIDAFTERNOON THE PROPHETS ARE STILL CALLING UPON BAAL TO SEND DOWN FIRE-- BUT THERE IS NO ANSWER. AT LAST THEY GIVE UP.

THEN ELIJAH BUILDS AN ALTAR TO GOD.

WHEN IT IS FINISHED, AND THE SACRIFICE PREPARED, ELIJAH ORDERS MEN TO POUR WATER OVER IT.

POUR ON MORE WATER. FILL THE TRENCH WITH IT.

THEN--BEFORE THE WATER-SOAKED ALTAR--ELIJAH PRAYS.

HEAR ME, O LORD, HEAR ME, THAT THE PEOPLE OF ISRAEL MAY KNOW THAT THOU ART THE LORD GOD.

Answer By Fire!

FROM I KINGS 18: 38—19: 2

FOR HOURS THE PROPHETS OF BAAL CALL UPON THEIR GOD TO PROVE HIMSELF BY SENDING FIRE -- BUT THERE IS NO ANSWER. THEN ELIJAH CALLS UPON GOD-- INSTANTLY FIRE SWEEPS DOWN AND BURNS UP NOT ONLY THE SACRIFICE, BUT THE ALTAR MADE OF STONES.

THE LORD... HE IS GOD!

THEN ELIJAH CLIMBS TO A PEAK ON THE MOUNTAIN TO PRAY. HE SENDS HIS SERVANT TO WATCH THE HORIZON.

GO UP A LITTLE HIGHER AND LOOK TOWARD THE SEA. TELL ME WHAT YOU SEE.

SIX TIMES THE SERVANT LOOKS OUT TOWARD THE SEA, AND REPORTS THAT HE SEES NOTHING. BUT WHEN ELIJAH SENDS HIM BACK THE SEVENTH TIME...

I SAW A CLOUD --NO LARGER THAN A MAN'S HAND.

RUN. TELL KING AHAB TO GET INTO HIS CHARIOT AND HURRY TO THE CITY BEFORE THE RAIN STOPS HIM.

ELIJAH IS SO EXCITED ABOUT HIS VICTORY OVER BAAL AND THE COMING RAIN THAT HE STARTS RUNNING FOR THE CITY. GOD GIVES HIM STRENGTH TO OUTRUN EVEN THE KING'S CHARIOT.

IN THE HOMES OF ISRAEL, THERE IS JOY-- THANKSGIVING -- AND REPENTANCE.

RAIN AT LAST! THE LORD BE PRAISED!

YES, IT WAS THE LORD WHO ANSWERED WITH FIRE! WE SHOULD NEVER HAVE WORSHIPED BAAL.

BUT IN THE PALACE QUEEN JEZEBEL IS FURIOUS...

WHEN THE PEOPLE SAW THE FIRE FROM GOD, THEY TURNED ON THE PROPHETS OF BAAL AND KILLED THEM. ELIJAH---

ELIJAH! ELIJAH! THAT'S ALL I HEAR! WELL, I'LL HEAR HIS NAME NO MORE!

SHE CALLS FOR A MESSENGER.

GO TO ELIJAH AND TELL HIM THAT BY THIS TIME TOMORROW HE WILL BE AS THOSE PROPHETS HE HAD PUT TO DEATH ON MOUNT CARMEL...

152

Voice in the Mountain

M I KINGS 19: 3-18

N A FIT OF RAGE
EEN JEZEBEL
ENDS WORD TO
LIJAH THAT HE
ILL BE PUT TO
EATH THE NEXT
AY. THAT NIGHT
LIJAH AND HIS
ERVANT MAKE
EIR ESCAPE.

WHERE CAN WE GO TO BE SAFE?

THE DESERT-- EVEN JEZEBEL WON'T LOOK FOR US THERE.

EIR JOURNEY TAKES
EM SOUTH THROUGH
RAEL AND JUDAH.
E SERVANT STAYS
THE CITY OF BEER-
HEBA, WHILE ELIJAH
ONTINUES ALONE INTO
E WILDERNESS. BUT
TER A DAY'S TRAVEL..

O LORD, TAKE MY LIFE. I HAVE DONE MY BEST TO BRING ISRAEL BACK TO THEE, BUT IT'S NO USE. THE PEOPLE WON'T LISTEN!

153

THEN, HUNGRY AND TIRED, ELIJAH FALLS ASLEEP. WHILE HE IS SLEEPING AN ANGEL APPEARS WITH BREAD AND WATER.

WAKE UP, ELIJAH, AND EAT.

ELIJAH IS ENCOURAGED BY THE FACT THAT GOD IS TAKING CARE OF HIM. AFTER HE EATS AND RESTS, HE CONTINUES HIS JOURNEY...

AND FORTY DAYS LATER HE REACHES MOUNT SINAI WHERE GOD TALKED TO MOSES.

I PRAY THAT I, TOO, MAY RECEIVE A MESSAGE FROM GOD ON THE MOUNTAIN.

SUDDENLY A GREAT STORM STRIKES. THE WIND HURLS ROCKS DOWN THE MOUNTAIN-- AN EARTHQUAKE SHAKES THE GROUND ON WHICH ELIJAH STANDS -- AND LIGHTNING SPLITS THE SKY! THE POWER OF GOD IS REVEALED IN THE STORM--BUT THERE IS NO MESSAGE.

THEN, IN THE QUIETNESS AFTER THE STORM, ELIJAH HEARS THE STILL, SMALL VOICE OF GOD.

ELIJAH, WHAT ARE YOU DOING HERE?

O LORD, THE PEOPLE OF ISRAEL DO NOT SERVE THEE. THEY WORSHIP IDOLS. THEY HAVE KILLED ALL OF YOUR OTHER PROPHETS--AND NOW THEY WANT TO KILL ME.

BUT GOD TELLS ELIJAH THERE IS WORK FOR HIM TO DO IN ISRAEL. --HIS COURAGE RENEWED-- ELIJAH STARTS BACK.

O GOD, I AM READY NOW TO FACE ANY DANGER.

Forged Letters

FROM I KINGS 19: 19-21; 21: 1-8

ELIJAH RETURNS TO ISRAEL TO SERVE AS GOD'S PROPHET. PASSING BY A FIELD HE STOPS AND THROWS HIS CLOAK OVER A YOUNG FARMER'S SHOULDERS.

ELIJAH! YOUR CLOAK! DOES THIS MEAN THAT YOU ARE CALLING **ME** TO BE A PROPHET?

YES, ELISHA, YOU HAVE BEEN APPOINTED BY GOD TO BE HIS SPOKESMAN IN ISRAEL.

WAIT--LET ME GO HOME AND SAY GOOD-BYE TO MY MOTHER AND FATHER; THEN I'LL GO WITH YOU.

OF COURSE--BUT JOIN ME SOON, FOR THERE IS WORK TO BE DONE FOR GOD.

SO ELISHA RETURNS HOME AND GIVES A FAREWELL FEAST FOR HIS FAMILY AND FRIENDS.

I KNOW, BUT GOD HAS CALLED ME, AND I MUST OBEY.

I'M PROUD OF YOU, SON.

YOU'RE GIVING UP A SAFE LIFE FOR A DANGEROUS ONE, ELISHA.

ELISHA GOES TO WORK WITH ELIJAH, AND WHILE THEY ARE TRAINING OTHER PROPHETS, KING AHAB MAKES A SURPRISE VISIT TO ONE OF HIS SUBJECTS.

NABOTH, I WANT TO BUY THIS VINEYARD. OR, IF YOU LIKE, I'LL GIVE YOU ANOTHER FOR IT.

I'M SORRY, O KING, BUT OUR FAMILY HAS OWNED THIS VINEYARD FOR MANY YEARS. IT WOULD NOT BE RIGHT TO SELL IT TO SOMEONE OUTSIDE THE FAMILY.

YOU MAY ALSO FIND THAT IT IS NOT RIGHT TO DISPLEASE YOUR KING!

LIKE A SPOILED CHILD WHO CANNOT HAVE HIS OWN WAY, AHAB RETURNS TO THE PALACE.

WHAT IS THE MATTER? ARE YOU ILL?

NO--I WANT NABOTH'S VINEYARD, BUT HE WON'T SELL IT TO ME!

WON'T? ARE YOU KING OF ISRAEL, OR AREN'T YOU?

BUT DON'T WORRY, I'LL GET THE VINEYARD FOR YOU.

QUICKLY JEZEBEL WRITES SOME LETTERS AND SIGNS THE KING'S NAME TO THEM.

DELIVER THESE TO THE ELDERS AND NOBLES OF THE CITY.

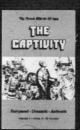